Venice: Discovering a Hidden Pathway

Marko Pogačnik

Venice: Discovering a Hidden Pathway

photographs by Bojan Brecelj

2008 / Lindisfarne Books

First published by Carucci editore, Rome, 1986.

Text and drawings copyright Marko Pogačnik 2008.

All Photographs, except those mentioned below, copyright Bojan Brecelj 2008.

Photographs on page 25: Arne Hodalic
Photographs on pages 239, 244, 249: courtesy of the Academy Galleries, Venice
Photographs on pages 39, 82, 119, 129, 160, 169, 184, 251: Osvaldo Bom, Venice

Published by Lindisfarne Books
610 Main Street, Great Barrington, Massachusetts 01230
www.lindisfarne.org

Library of Congress Cataloging-in-Publication Data is available.

ISBN: 978 158420 0550

to Paolo, the Venetian Master:
was it your idea to create Venice?

Acknowledgments

I am grateful to Gene Gollogly and all those at Lindisfarne Books for saving my dear book *Venice* from total oblivion by publishing it again after 21 years. It seems to have been published too far ahead of its time in 1986, when unfortunate circumstances in the world blocked its way to reaching the public. With today's newborn interest in the health of the Earth and its waters and atmosphere, this is the right moment for *Venice* to enter our consciousness with the inspiration of how to create a city in harmony with the elements of Earth and Cosmos.

Since this book was first published in 1986 I have written two more books on Venice, one in German (*Geheimnis Venedig*) and the other in Italian (*Venezia invisible*), trying to communicate the importance of Venice for the Earth's equilibrium. The city of Venice has been erected on one of the major balancing centers of the planet. As a consequence, the disharmonies that one can perceive in Venice mirror the state of our modern world with all its imbalances. But also, I believe, if the true essence of Venice is properly understood and supported, it will contribute to the balance of the earth energy fields.

My deep thanks goes to anthropologists Allison and Marek Jablonko, who enthusiastically took part in my early workshops in Venice (1979-86), making it possible for such a beautiful book to appear today. My appreciation also goes to Bojan Brecelj, dear friend and photographer, who again and again followed in my footsteps, taking pictures in the very moment new insights into the organism of Venice were opening to me.

Marko Pogačnik
EASTER 2007

Contents

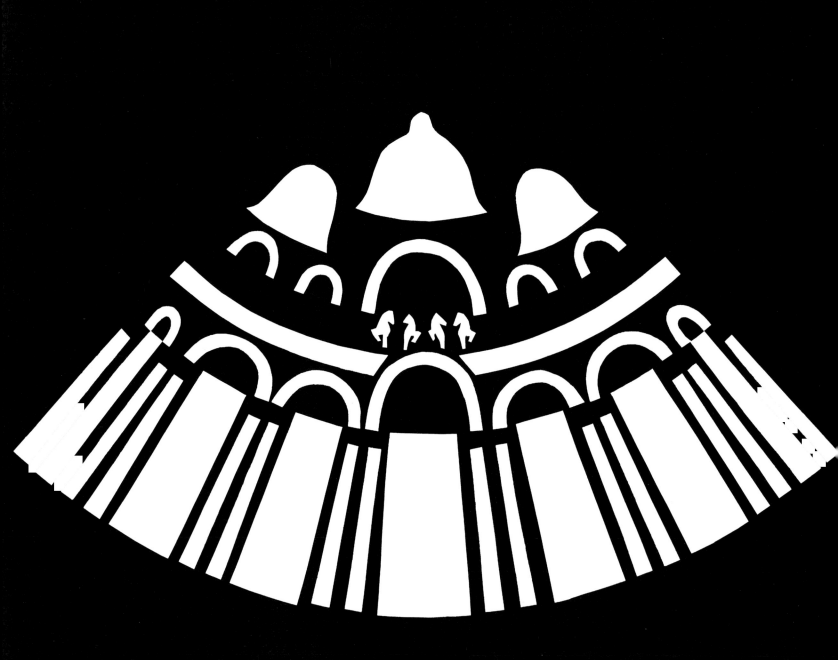

Introduction

Today we are predominantly an urban civilization. We center our intellectual activity and the greatest of our artistic creations in the cities, whirlpools of intense life. Yet we are not happy in these cities. When we identify with them, we feel cut off from our true selves. Is it the *cities* that are damaging our humanity, or are we doing violence to our cities by using them solely as functional frameworks and by exhibiting them as historical showplaces?

Years of working in the city of Venice lead me to believe that human consciousness is the essential factor in this dilemma. What we see and experience around us has, to a large extent, been molded within our consciousness and projected outwards as the visible world within which we move. This world, which we call objective reality, others, such as the Buddhists, call subjective illusion. I would not call this world simply illusion, for it is a true expression of our consciousness at any given point in our evolution. Neither would I accept it as the ultimate reality, since I am convinced that our life offers greater freedom to choose, to be, and to create than is generally supposed.

Given the rapidity with which rational thought has developed during the last two centuries, I can understand why, today, we find ourselves in a world in which we analyze everything in the minutest detail. On the other hand, we have largely lost the ability to recognize the unity of all things within the universe and the intimate place each one of us occupies in it. In this unbalanced situation it is not surprising that I feel drawn to the very opposite of the rational, to the intuitive realm. Here, the separation of subject from object ceases to exist; the structure of space, which constantly separates the personal psychic world from the worlds of other beings and other dimensions, tends to be transcended; the boundaries of time are lifted, and the message of the past becomes relevant for the present.

Yet I do not use the intuitive path to the exclusion of the rational. I find that, within ourselves, we have the capability of treading both paths in equilibrium. I have called this intertwined path "hidden" in the title of this book because, indeed, it remains invisible until we begin to complement rational modes of perception with our intuitive insights.

I have purposely chosen Venice as the city scape through which to trace a "hidden pathway" because Venice was so obviously built upon the balance of two contrasting elements, water and earth. In Venice any part of the city can be reached both by water and by land. For me this is symbolic of exploring any reality following both intuitive and rational paths.

The first step in the process of tracing this pathway through Venice has been personal dialogue. I approached each location, building, and painting again and again in inner peace and attunement, sometimes using dowsing techniques to sharpen my sensitivity to the energy currents of a given space. I carefully articulated the inspirations received in response, using the tools proper to the "science of intuition," such as the classical concept of the four elements, the Chinese concept of yin and yang, and the alchemical concept of creation as the wedding of the feminine and masculine aspects — tools which belong to the traditions of diverse cultures and epochs of human evolution.

The second step in the process was to formulate the findings in such a way that they could be understood on the rational plane. I was seeking evidence of the intuited reality on the outer physical level, for example in the formal structure of architecture, in the composition of paintings, and in historical records. Further, I was looking for instances where my findings would be meaningful for us today, helping us to know more about ourselves, and supporting us in our present quest to find our place within the cosmic whole.

Finally, the book itself has been created in the form of a micro city, the design of the book corresponding to the dual structure of Venice. The mental quality of the text is balanced by the emotional quality of the line drawings and the photographs, just as the "hard" streets of Venice are balanced by the "soft" waters of the canals. To embody the role of bridges in the book, I have created special black and white diagrams which combine mental clarity with visual immediacy, linking the text with the line drawings and photographs.

In the beginning, I mentioned that may we distort a city by turning it into a mere historical show place. To a great extent this has happened to Venice. I believe that the healing process starts with a clear reaffirmation of a city's lost identity. I hope that this book will help to uncover the deeper layers of the present city so that a new cycle of growth may sprout from those depths.

The scene, then, is set for another Venice. I invite You to step in.

Marko Pogačnik

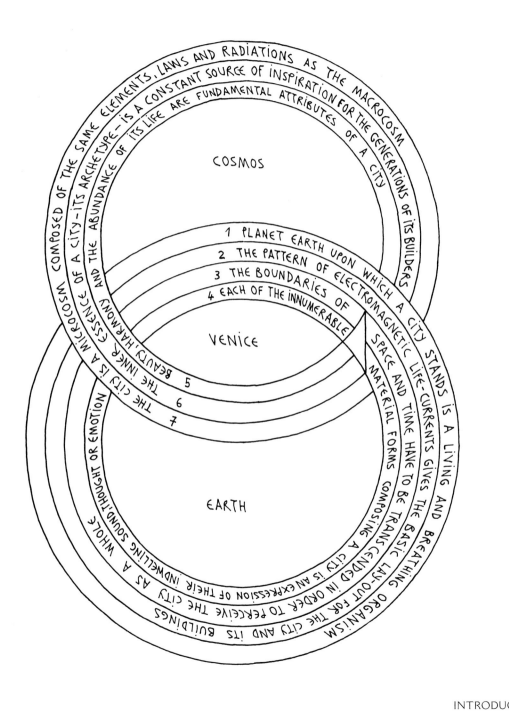

COSMOS

COMPOSED OF THE SAME ELEMENTS, LAWS AND RADIATIONS AS THE MACROCOSM—IS A CONSTANT SOURCE OF INSPIRATION FOR THE GENERATIONS OF ITS BUILDERS

OF A CITY—ITS ARCHETYPE—THE ABUNDANCE OF ITS LIFE ARE FUNDAMENTAL ATTRIBUTES OF A CITY

AND THE MICROCOSM OF A CITY—ITS ARCHETYPE—IS THE INNER ESSENCE OF A CITY

BEAUTY, HARMONY

1 PLANET EARTH UPON WHICH A CITY STANDS IS A LIVING AND BREATHING ORGANISM

2 THE PATTERN OF ELECTROMAGNETIC LIFE-CURRENTS GIVES THE BASIC LAY-OUT FOR THE CITY AND ITS BUILDINGS

3 THE BOUNDARIES OF SPACE AND TIME HAVE TO BE TRANSCENDED IN ORDER TO PERCEIVE THE CITY AS A WHOLE

4 EACH OF THE INNUMERABLE MATERIAL FORMS COMPOSING A CITY IS AN EXPRESSION OF THEIR INDWELLING SOUND, THOUGHT OR EMOTION

5

6

7 THE CITY IS A MICROCOSM

VENICE

EARTH

THE CORE OF VENICE

The City as a Whole

1

Before we enter the city and plunge into its microcosm, let us look at it from above, as if looking at a map. The ground plan of Venice is shaped like a fish. The head is the area of the Santa Lucia railway station; the wide open jaws are the mouth of the Grand Canal. The belly of the fish rounds off at Giudecca Canal, while its back is outlined by the Fondamenta Nuove. Its body becomes narrower behind Saint Mark's Square and then extends into a two pronged tail. The city has developed a shape complementary to its water nature: the shape of a water creature.

1. "The ground plan of Venice is shaped like a fish."

2. Venice is built around a water axis: the Grand Canal.

3

3. "The city's energy, in the form of goods and passenger traffic..."

The fish shape is an appropriate image for the city of Venice. The city's energy, in the form of goods and passenger traffic, flows into the open jaws of the fish. Here the road and railway enter the city and here is the port for cargo ships. In the tail of the fish the Venetian Navy was stationed. The Venetian fleet was the means by which the city could reach into the larger world, just as the tail propels a fish through the sea.

This external form of Venice is thought-provoking. However, one may ask whether the fish shape is significant in terms of the inner life of the city.

The open mouth of the fish is one end of the Grand Canal, which meanders through the city and ends beside Saint Mark's Square. Looking at the Canal on a map, we can imagine it as a backbone that runs from the head downward. Just as the human body grows around a solid axis, the backbone, the body of Venice is built around a water axis. It should not disturb us that the water axis of Venice meanders, for the human backbone is not straight either: both are curved in the shape of the letter "S."

4

4. The water axis of Venice meanders through the city.

5. The human backbone is also curved in the shape of the letter "S."

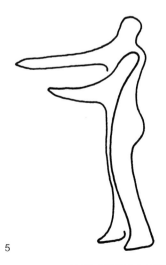

5

The Grand Canal, as the city's water axis, links two significant points of Venice. At one end, the railway and bus stations and a parking area are clustered. Here we are obliged to leave our "terrestrial" vehicles in exchange for water transport. At the other end, the city center is anchored by Saint Mark's Basilica, the Doges' Palace, and the City Portal. Here we experience the spiritual and historic core of Venice.

Now let us look at the Grand Canal as the backbone of Venice. Our own backbone connects the two dominant points of our body. On the head are gathered the links we need for communication with our environment: eyes, mouth and ears. Venice's links with the environment — railway, road, and port — are gathered in a similar way at the beginning of the Grand Canal. At the base of the human backbone, the second dominant point is anchored. Here the human being is conceived and new life is born. Similarly at the end of the Canal, in Saint Mark's Basilica, the Doges' Palace, and the administrative buildings, decisions affecting the life of Venice were made.

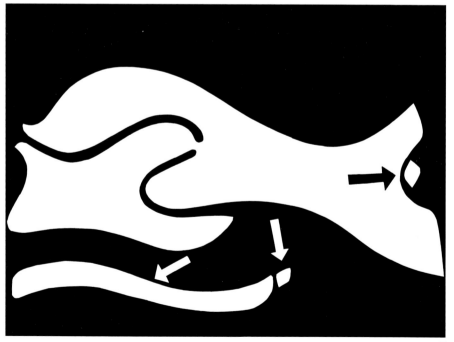

6. The City Portal.

7. "The Grand Canal, as the city's water axis, links two significant points of Venice."

8

8. "Our own backbone connects the two dominant points of our body."

9. The interlacing of the city roofs seen from Saint Mark's Bell Tower.

9

In addition to the two dominant points at the beginning and the end of the Canal, there is a third important point: the Rialto Bridge which crosses its center. It is the only traditional bridge spanning the Grand Canal, the only solid link between the two parts of the city. (The bridges at the railway station and the Academy were erected recently.) What, then, is the significance of the Rialto in relation to the backbone of Venice?

The backbone is in fact only the physical counterpart of a much more subtle body axis along which are distributed the energy centers — on the physical level known as endocrine glands — which chart the life processes of the human organism. We have mentioned two of these energy centers in connection with both ends of the Grand Canal. A third dominant point, the midpoint of this subtle body axis, is reflected on the human figure by the navel.

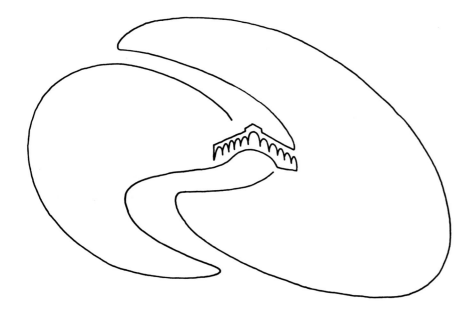

10

10. If we could hold Venice by the Rialto Bridge, we would be holding it at its point of balance.

The navel is not only a reminder of the original link with the mother, through which we were fed our first vital energies, but it is also the geometric center of the human body. If we draw a circle around the human figure, the navel is at its center. Just as the navel is at the center of the human being, the Rialto Bridge is placed at the gravity center of Venice.

The Rialto vaults above the Grand Canal like a semicircular handle of a vessel. If we could hold Venice by this handle and lift it high into the air, the city would not tilt or fall to pieces for we would be holding it at its point of balance.

11

11. "If we draw a circle around the human figure, the navel is at its center.

12

With all this in mind, we can say that the city of Venice is a fish-human organism: its outer form is shaped in the semblance of the fish, its inner counterpart relates to the human constitution. Interestingly enough, fish-men appear in the mythologies of ancient Egyptian, Mesopotamian, and Greek cultures as divine beings.

The fish human figure is an appropriate representation of this city, which is not only surrounded by water, being situated in the middle of the lagoon, but is also permeated by water in the form of numerous canals. Solid ground hardly seems to exist in Venice: nature is present only as water nature. All this corresponds to the fish part of the symbol.

12. "Solid ground hardly seems to exist in Venice."

The human part of the figure corresponds to the city's architectural structure: urban units held together by numerous bridges. Placed just above the surface of the sea, this structure appears as a totally human creation.

Characteristically, the portals of the Venetian palaces are reached by stairs leading directly out of the sea, as if one day water creatures might be expected as guests.

13

13. "The portals of the Venetian palaces are reached by stairs leading directly out of the sea."

14. "Fish-men appear in the mythologies of ancient Egyptian, Mesopotamian, and Greek cultures as divine beings."

14

The City Portal

The water nature of Venice is so dominant that even today, when we usually approach from the mainland, the City Portal is still located to welcome our arrival by water, whether along the Grand Canal or from the Adriatic Sea. Since waterways are always open, the Venetian Portal is not in the customary form of ancient city gates. The practical function of the gates is abandoned. What is retained is the symbolic aspect which reminds us that we are standing in front of a complex being called "The City."

15

15. "The water nature of Venice is so dominant that even today ... The City Portal is still located to welcome our arrival by water ..."

The Portal is formed by two monolithic columns standing opposite one another on the edge of Saint Mark's Little Square. The granite columns were brought from an ancient temple, possibly Egyptian, during the twelfth century. The tremendous power of the stone may be experienced by approaching and touching them.

Each column is crowned by an animal: the dragon of Saint Theodore and the winged lion of Saint Mark. These animals are placed in such a way that their tails shoot toward one another, as if each column were a source of electric power: negative on the left, positive on the right. Since both sculptures are standing on unusually wide bases, the bodies of the animals are concealed when we approach them: one can see only the two tails resembling energy sparks that dart toward each other. The energy current which runs between the two tails forms the invisible lintel, the horizontal part of the gate.

16

16. Saint Mark's Little Square in the early morning.

17. "One can see only the two tall tails resembling energy
sparks that dart toward each other."

The nature of each animal plays a significant part in the role of the Portal. The dragon, its rigid body pressed toward the ground, embodies *terrestrial powers*, which have slow vibrations and gravitate downward. Its tail, covered with heavy scaly matter, seems to wave slowly. It symbolizes the negative energy pole of the left-hand column.

18

18. "The dragon, its rigid body pressed toward the ground, embodies terrestrial powers ..."

The lion standing on the column charged with
positive energy almost floats on air with its
wings. It embodies the *cosmic powers*, which have
fast vibrations and strive upward. The elegantly
waving tail ends in a tuft of flame-energy.

Spirit and matter are the two poles through
which creation on our planet evolves. Their
symbols, facing each other on the Portal columns
of Venice, indicate that one is entering a city
created by both terrestrial and cosmic forces.

19

19. "The lion standing on the column charged with positive
energy almost floats on air with its wings."

Saint Mark's Basilica

20

Beyond the Venetian Portal we enter Saint Mark's Square where we shall pause for a moment to let the image of the Basilica fill us. A vast energy radiates from the Basilica. This energy does not rise upward as in Gothic cathedrals, nor does it harmonize in classic relationships as in Renaissance churches. The Basilica's energy spreads horizontally: its width is greater than its height. The arches above the entrances and above the lunettes on the first floor do not strive upward, but, being wide, rise gently to form two horizontal, wavy lines. Between the ground floor and the first floor a straight balcony line is drawn across the whole width of the building, thus underlining its horizontal nature.

20. "The Basilica's energy spreads horizontally ..."

21. The façade of Saint Mark's Basilica could be related to a seascape.

22

The foundations of Saint Mark's Basilica stand only slightly above sea level and, when high tide invades the Square, the Basilica seems to float on the water. Just as Gothic cathedrals may be related to mountain peaks, we could say that the Basilica of Saint Mark is related to a seascape.

If we were to search in nature for the forms present on the Basilica's façade, we would find them only in the sea. The wealth of carved and gilded marble and the many elaborate shapes of colored mosaic could look almost garish to someone unaware that they reflect patterns and shapes created by the sea.

We might imagine that the Basilica was built on the sea bed and, thanks to the. skills of many generations of Venetian masters, it gradually rose from the waters to rest just above the surface of the sea. Even today, it may remind us of a coral reef with intricate branching columns, colorful sea anemones, and spiral algae.

22. "The wealth of carved and gilded marble ... reflect patterns and shapes created by the sea."

23. "When high tide invades the Square, the Basilica seems to float on the water."

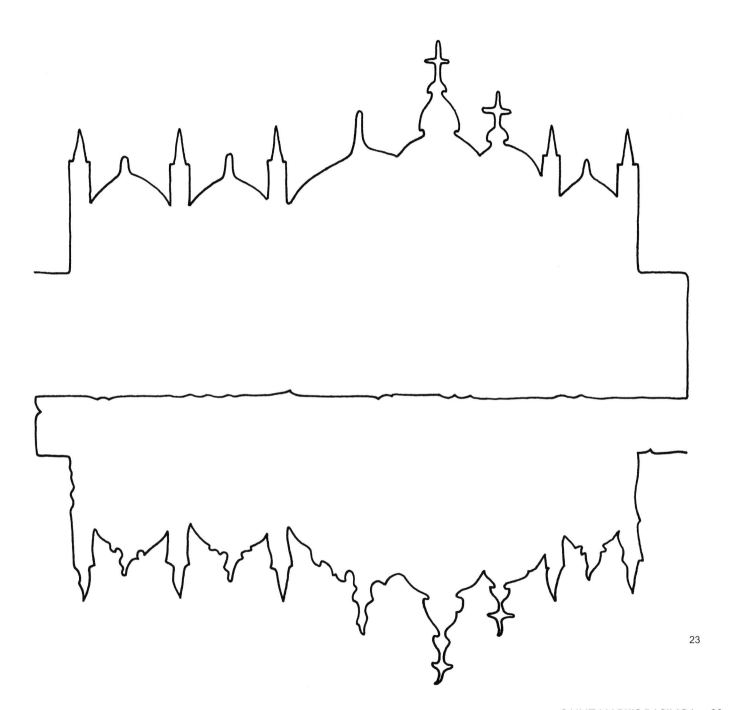

23

24

24. The cupolas of Saint Mark's Basilica dominate the "watercity."

25. A corner of Saint Mark's seen from the Bell Tower
may remind us of a coral reef.

The horizontal line of the balcony is interrupted at one point only. This dominant point of the façade, above the main entrance, is marked by four bronze horses — a Greek work of art dating from the fourth century B.C.

What is the meaning of the four horses placed at the central point of a façade otherwise adorned by sacred Christian images?

They evoke the memory of the Greek myth of Helios (the Sun) traveling in his chariot across the sky. The chariot is pulled by four horses representing the four elements — fire, water, air, earth — that draw universal creation through cycles of evolution.

The four horses remind us that Saint Mark's is not only a Christian church, but is also a universal sanctuary, meaningful to whoever turns within to find the cosmic depths of life.

26

26. "Four horses representing the four elements — fire, water, air, earth — that draw universal creation through cycles of evolution."

27

In harmony with its façade, the interior of the Basilica is reminiscent of a water environment. If you have ever skin-dived, you will know how the surface of the sea glitters in the Sun when seen from below. In the Basilica, the ceiling, completely covered with gold mosaics, glitters above us in the same manner.

The light enters Saint Mark's through small openings around the bases of the cupolas and under the side arches, illuminating the mosaics above and leaving the lower portions in darkness. The effects of light in the depths of the sea are similar: the deeper layers are in darkness, while the top layer is bathed in dazzling brightness. Inside Saint Mark's Basilica we feel as if we are standing at the bottom of the sea.

The marble slabs of the walls are arranged symmetrically, which allows the design of their veins to recall the rhythmic reflections of light playing on the surface of waves. Even the floor of the Basilica seems to undulate.

27. "The effects of light in the depths of the sea are similar: the deeper layers are in darkness."

28. "The top layer is bathed in dazzling brightness."

29

We could therefore call Saint Mark's Basilica a "water sanctuary" in the same way that we have called Venice a "water city," although each has its own particular relationship to water. The city uses water in a practical way, as a means of communication. The sanctuary, on the other hand, embodies water as an ideal, as a cosmic element.

It would be impossible for Venice to pulsate for centuries, radiating its energy, and at the same time to retain its identity, unless it had a sanctuary that could preserve pure and unchanging the inherent pattern of the water element. It is from Saint Mark's that the city has, throughout the centuries, been absorbing the essence of the water element and has, accordingly, created its "water form."

In return, throughout the same centuries, the city has been pouring into the Basilica the human energy of worship and love and also its material wealth: the most valuable of its war trophies and other treasures. The city and its sanctuary are linked by an unbroken flow of energy. Both have grown simultaneously, both becoming increasingly beautiful.

30 ▶

29. "The marble slabs of the walls ... recall the rhythmic reflections of light playing on the surface of waves."

30. "The city and its sanctuary are linked by an unbroken flow of energy."

31. The finely worked mosaic floor, reflecting the sunlight, evokes images of the watery sea-bed.

32. "Even the floor of the Basilica seems to undulate."

32

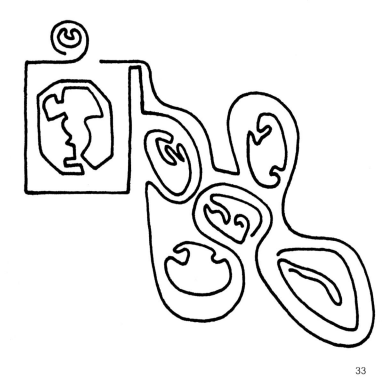

33

Surprisingly, the Basilica's most valuable artistic expression may not be related to the water, but to the fire element. Let us look behind the main altar at the Golden Altar Plate (Pala d'oro) with its innumerable enamel miniatures and precious stones. The first part of the Plate was ordered by Doge Pietro Orseolo I (976-978) in Constantinople. But it was not until 1345, when Andrea Dandolo held the office of Doge, that the Plate was completed. Originally it was not intended to be looked at, as it is today, when the Altar Plate can be visited as part of the Basilica's treasury, for its real importance does not lie in its outer material worth and aesthetic splendor.

Imagine that in our universe innumerable tiny threads of energy and mental currents are intermingled. Certain of the resulting vibrations are necessary to promote a city's growth. With the help of the extremely delicate precious stones and metals, and through the scenes and characters of the Christian tradition, the Golden Altar Plate attracts, retains and radiates those valuable currents. The most sacred location in Venice, the one behind the main altar of Saint Mark's Basilica, is an appropriate location for the city's direct contact with what we could call "the cosmic fire."

33. A detail from the Golden Altar Plate illustrating the elaborate interplay of the precious stones and metals.

In the cupola close to the entrance we see a mosaic with an extraordinary radial design. At the top appears the fire of the Holy Spirit — the unlimited source of Life. From this source twelve energy currents run to the heads of the twelve Apostles seated in a circle around the bottom of the cupola. On the strip below them are representatives of all the peoples of the earth known at the time the Basilica was built.

Human beings are presented in pairs, always a woman and a man together. The twelve Apostles stand beyond this dualistic world and appear as unitary figures, each directly linked by a thread of energy to the cosmic source of Life. They depict the "higher" selves of the common people below them, who, even though immersed in the world of duality and matter, are linked to the source of all Good through their own spiritual selves.

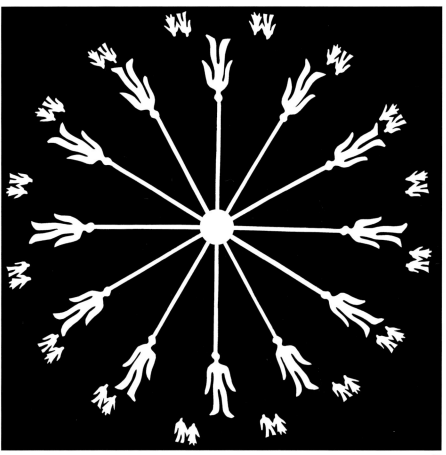

34

34. A rendering of the radial design in the cupola near the entrance.

35. The Golden Altar Plate, the city's direct contact with the cosmic fire, occupies the most sacred location in Venice — behind the main altar within Saint Mark's Basilica.

36. The energies radiating from the Golden Altar Plate
are transmitted through the Basilica's structure into the
entire city.

37. In preserving the relics of the saints, the sanctuary and the city continue to maintain contact with their energies.

In the treasury we can find yet another link between Saint Mark's Basilica and the more elusive realities of life. A large collection of relics is preserved in the chapel to the left. We catch our breath when we look at such skillfully shaped vessels containing skulls, thigh-bones, hair, etc., of women and men of the past who developed ordinary human qualities to such a point that they were proclaimed saints. The energy that built up throughout their lives is not lost, for energy is indestructible. In preserving their remains and the objects they used, the sanctuary and the city continue to maintain contact with these energies and to draw inspiration from them for their own growth and development.

38

38. A chalice from the treasury of Saint Mark's Basilica.

Saint Mark's Square

39

Stepping out of Saint Mark's Basilica, where we had gradually become aware of effects recalling the *water element* and the *fire element*, we enter Saint Mark's Square. We now encounter entirely different elements. Here are the famous pigeons which were brought centuries ago from Cyprus and have since then dwelt in the Square. Suddenly a flock rises up and swirls the air around our heads, as though the pigeons are here to remind us, time and again, of the *air element*.

Framing the Square are the buildings called the "Procuratie," once the administrative seat of the Venetian Republic. Their rigorous classical form and the crystalline structure of the façade convey an impression of the *earth element*. Even the functions performed within them — responsibility for law, finance, and property — were "earthly" in nature.

The full meaning of the four horses on the Basilica's façade now becomes apparent. Embodying the four elements — water, fire, air, earth — they stand at the dominant point of the Square, as its symbol of identity.

39. "Here are the famous pigeons which were brought centuries ago from Cyprus."

40. "The pigeons are here to remind us, time and again, of the *air element*."

40

40

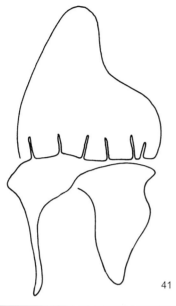

41

After the fall of the Venetian Republic, the administrative buildings were partly taken over by the Correr Museum, which now preserves them for their historical interest. The museum houses a ceremonial head covering (corno ducale) of the Republic's leader, the Doge.

The original function of a ruler's head-covering was to exalt his wisdom as the guarantee of the State's prosperity. By setting the greatest wealth of their state in their crowns, many rulers substituted the quality of wisdom with personal power. The law of the Venetian Republic did not allow for such a transformation: in contrast to the bejeweled crowns worn by many kings and rulers of that period, the Doge's head-covering was made of simple cloth and remained the same throughout the duration of the Republic. The lower part of the head-covering clings tightly to the skull and ears, accentuating the head as the seat of the human intellect. And since the human intellect is limited, the upper part of the head-covering rises above the head, in the shape of a horn, and evokes wisdom as a quality superior to the power of the individual personality.

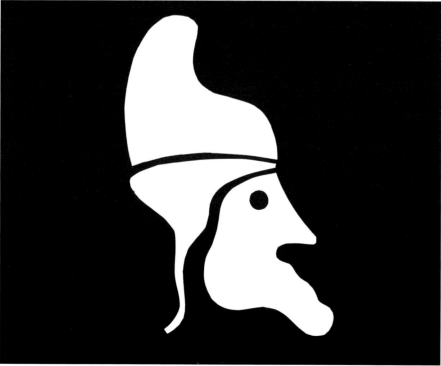

41. A doge's head-covering is preserved in the Correr Museum.

42. The head-covering rises above the head as a symbol of wisdom.

42

43. The rigorous classical form and the crystalline structure of the facades around Saint Mark's Square convey an impression of the earth element.

The Clock Tower

Looking at the city's ground plan from above, we discovered that Venice is aligned along a "water axis" which meanders through the city as the Grand Canal. This water axis is supplemented by an "earth axis."

By axis we do not mean a straight line but a stream of energy along which the main functions of the city are distributed and the prominent buildings have been concentrated. The energy of an axis has its origin in one of the many energy streams of the Earth's electromagnetic field. These energy streams may extend over great distances and the position of an axis lies along a segment of one of them. Throughout the centuries the energy of any axis has been reinforced by that of the people continually moving along it.

44. Venice's earth axis passes beneath the Clock Tower.

The urban fabric of Venice was established upon water as well as upon earth and, accordingly, evolved along two axes. Most of the water traffic moves along the Grand Canal, Venice's water axis, while the main stream of pedestrians moves along the city's earth axis.

Venice's earth axis begins to gather its momentum of energy at the edge of Saint Mark's Little Square between the two Portal columns, crosses Saint Mark's Square passing along the façade of the Basilica, and heads straight through the passage beneath the Clock Tower (Torre dell' Orologio). From here it runs through a number of narrow streets, called the "Mercerie," and crosses the Rialto Bridge into the market place, Venice's ancient center of commerce.

45. Above the earth axis the clock marks the cycles of earthly time.

45

46

The "Mercerie," a succession of narrow streets lined with the city's most elegant shops, embody the practical aspect of the city's earth axis. Along these small streets people rush to and fro engaged in their "earthly" pursuits. Above the city's earth axis stands the Clock Tower marking earthly time. The Clock Tower is a most appropriate portal for this earth axis. On its top stand the bronze sculptures of two Moors who strike the bell with their hammers as the time passes. The large clock on the façade shows the phases of the Moon and the movement of the Sun in relation to the twelve signs of the zodiac.

As we leave Saint Mark's, a place dedicated to spirituality, we are leaving the eternal dimension. We enter the commercial thoroughfares — the area of the city in which time rules supreme. Here minutes and hours flow by, the Sun and the Moon move in their orbits, and the cycle of our earthly life from birth to death runs its course.

47 ▶

46. On top of the Clock Tower the bronze sculptures of two Moors strike the bell.

47. "The large clock on the façade shows the movement of the Sun in relation to the twelve signs of the zodiac."

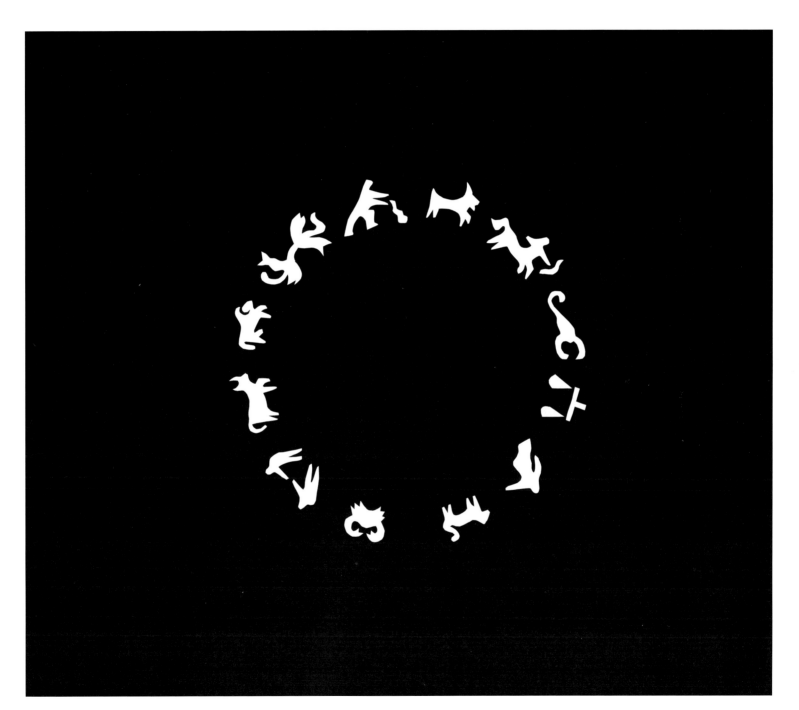

48

48. The earth axis runs through the narrow streets of the "Mercerie."

49. "The Mercerie," lined with the city's most elegant shops, embodies the practical aspect of the city's earth axis.

The Doges' Palace

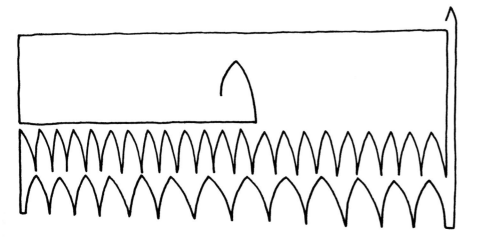

50

Saint Mark's Basilica and the Doges' Palace are linked, and together they make up the spiritual and historic core of the city. They do not, however, face each other, but each opens on its respective square. The Bell Tower stands guard between the two squares, as if to keep the historic nature of the square in front of the Doges' Palace separate from the spiritual nature of the square in front of Saint Mark's Basilica.

51 ▶

50. The Gothic rhythms of the Doges' Palace.

51. The Bell Tower stands guard between the two squares.

Saint Mark's Basilica, with its spiritual-artistic structure, is dedicated to forces which function constantly through eons of time: questions concerning the ultimate source and meaning of life, which are as relevant today as they were millennia ago. In contrast to the energies operating in the Basilica, those in the Doges' Palace had their source in the Venetian Republic, which flourished during the astrological age of Pisces.

The nature of the energies of the Doges' Palace is directly connected with the rise and fall of the Piscean age. The feeling of emptiness the visitor experiences in the interior of the Palace is in keeping with this astrological context. Within its spacious rooms with their opulently embellished walls, one feels as if the vital life forces have drained away.

52

52. The visitor experiences a feeling of emptiness in the interior of the Palace.

53. The energies present in the Doges' Palace flourished during the astrological age of Pisces.

53

We have met the zodiacal signs already on the Clock Tower. They represent the greater time cycle, approximately twenth-four thousand years long, within which our solar system moves. It is analogous to the one year cycle within which our Earth orbits. According to Plato, each of the twelve time sequences of the solar cycle lasts about two millennia and is governed by the energy force characteristic of the corresponding zodiacal constellation. With the ending of the present millennium, for example, the Piscean age of the solar cycle is drawing to its close, and the Aquarian age is beginning to unfold.

54. The arches of the Doges' Palace convey the upward striving aspect of the Piscean Age.

54

55

56

How do we detect the traces of this Piscean energy in the architectural structure of the Doges' Palace? The Palace has to be regarded as a complex together with the "Palace of Jails" (Palazzo delle Carceri) on the other side of the canal "della Paglia." On one side of the canal stands the Palace, full of gold and luxury; on the other side the jails, filled with misery and darkness. The two extremes are linked by the famous Bridge of Sighs (Ponte dei Sospiri), across which the condemned were led from the hall of justice to the jail. The shape of the sign of Pisces is similar: two fish linked by a narrow ribbon. The fish represent two extremes pushing away from each other, while the ribbon represents the force that unites them. Characteristically, the visitor's path through the Doges' Palace leads first through the richly painted rooms, then across the Bridge of Sighs into the miserable, bare jails, tracing the development of the energies present in it which once were vital and then dwindled with time.

55. "The Palace has to be regarded as a complex together with the 'Palace of Jails' on the other side of the canal 'della Paglia'."

56. "The two extremes are linked by the famous Bridge of Sighs."

The tragic dual nature of the Doges' Palace itself is not apparent from outside. It turns to the public its ceremonial face, which is nevertheless also divided into two distinctly contrasting levels. The lower part of the building is hollowed out — by the arcades of the ground floor and the loggia of the second floor — and fragmented by sculptural ornamentation. The upper part is as plain and smooth as a flat, square stone.

Surprisingly, none of the Palace façades has accentuated doors. This is rare in the architecture of that period, when portals were prominent. Of course, the Doges' Palace has its entrance, but this is placed well to the side, in a sort of wing between the Palace and the Basilica. This door is called the "Porta della Carta," literally "the paper door."

57. The balcony is the opening through which the Palace communicates with its environment.

57

58

In place of portals, two balconies are accentuated on its façades. Their central position and sculptural elaboration indicate that they are the opening through which the Palace communicates with its environment. On a ship like the Venetian galley, one does not communicate through a door either, but across a deck. The same applies to the Doges' Palace: one does not communicate through the portal, but across the two balconies. When the Doge appeared on one of the balconies, he in effect stood on the ship's deck.

This architectural form is in keeping with the function of the Palace. In its halls the Doge and the aldermen of Venice took decisions on how to lead, govern and defend their "water republic." Poetically speaking, they steered the Venetian ship across the rough seas of history.

58. The palace turns its ceremonial face to the public.

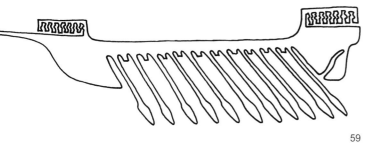

59. "On a ship like the Venetian galley one does not communicate through a door either, but across a deck."

60. The ceremonial face of the Palace is divided into two contrasting levels.

61

61. The "Giants' Staircase" in the inner courtyard of the Palace.

When we enter the inner courtyard through the "paper door," we are disappointed, for we do not have the sensation of a ship. Instead, the feeling is one of standing on firm ground.

The Doges' Palace again manifests its dual nature. The sense of dry land prevails because of the rational concept of the sixteenth-century court-yard designed by the Renaissance masters.

Each part of the courtyard is treated as an individual entity worthy of special attention. Let us take, for example, the "Giants' Staircase" (Scala dei Giganti) named after the large sculptures of Neptune and Mars by Jacopo Sansovino, which stand at the top. The vertical plane of each step is inlaid with a different ornament!

62. Some of the ornaments adorning the risers of the "Giants' Staircase."

62

63. Imagine that these paintings constitute the Palace's sails billowed out by the airy dynamics of the gilded ceilings.

Entering the Palace halls, we are impressed by the huge canvases which cover the ceilings and the walls. Recalling the image of the ship, imagine that these paintings constitute the Palace's sails billowed out by the airy dynamics of the gilded ceilings.

When we evoke the image of sails, we do not merely imply poetic parable. On these "sails" are painted the forces that propelled the ship of the Venetian Republic through history. Here are portrayed the decisive moments of its growth, such as the battle of Lepanto. Allegories of the moral values which Venice wished to weave into its ambience are depicted through ancient mythological scenes. The forces that work from beyond the horizons of human consciousness are denoted by scenes taken from Christian iconography.

64. A sixteenth-century Venetian galleon.

64

Two examples of this can be found in the "Sala dell'Anticollegio." In former times ambassadors and delegations waited here to be received by the governing body, the "Signoria." Which energies did the Palace wish to display to the waiting men?

On the right side of the door we find Jacopo Tintoretto's painting "Pallas rejecting Mars." Pallas Athena represents wisdom. Mars represents war. With her left hand Wisdom is rejecting War; with her right hand she is embracing Peace-Abundance. This was also the policy adopted by the Venetian Republic, which preferred to gain its victories through wise diplomacy rather than military force.

65

65. "Pallas rejecting Mars," after the painting by Jacopo Tintoretto.

*The next wall is adorned with "The Rape of Europa"
by Paolo Veronese.* This painting represents the
origin of European civilization. The Zeus–bull
has humbly lain down in order that the maiden,
the beautiful Europa, could sit on his back.
The bull represents the wild, primitive peoples
who overran Europe after the fall of the Roman
Empire. By the Middle Ages, these people had
developed a distinctive culture, which was later
labeled "Gothic" by the Renaissance masters,
as they equated it with the barbarism of the
Goths. Just as Zeus fell in love with the maiden,
people "fell in love" with the classical Greco-
Roman culture at the end of the Middle Ages.
The triangle rising in the background above the
maiden's head denotes her classical origin. The
new European culture — the Renaissance —
sprang up as a synthesis of the ancient classical
culture and the "barbarian" medieval culture.
This synthesis is evoked on the painting by
Europa touching the hind leg of the bull with
her toes and the base of the triangle with her
head, thus uniting the twin sources of European
culture.

66. "The Rape of Europa," after the painting by Paoto
Veronese.

67

When we enter the next hall, the "Sala del Collegio," we stand in front of the Doge's throne. It is amazingly simple. The only striking feature is a powerful *triangle* extending above the seat. The hall was designed by the architect Andrea Palladio, upon whose work we shall concentrate later. If we look across the bay in front of the Doges' Palace, we notice two further masterpieces by the same architect, their façades also crowned by triangles. The first is the Basilica of San Giorgio Maggiore standing on the island of the same name; the second, the Redentore Basilica, is on the island of Giudecca.

68

67. "The only striking feature is a powerful triangle extending above the seat."

68. The Basilica of San Giorgio Maggiore is crowned with a similar triangle.

69. Saint Mark's Basin, the "water square" of Venice,
extends from the Basilica of San Giorgio Maggiore on
the left to the Salute Basilica on the right.

70. The tower of "Dogana de Mar" with the Salute Basilica
in the background.

It is fitting that Venice, the "water city," has a "water square," which is enclosed by these monuments. Its sea surface, known as Saint Mark's Basin (Bacino di San Marco), is a counterpart to the terrestrial surface of Saint Mark's Square. Just as the latter is dominated by the four horses, a cosmic symbol, the Basin, too, has its crowning symbol, a golden sphere positioned above a building called the "Dogana da Mar." On the sphere a bronze figure of Fortune rotates according to the direction of the wind. In contrast to the celestial nature of the four horses, however, this is a profane symbol denoting the changing fortune of earthly life.

Saint Mark's Basin also holds a secret: a third portal column which was swallowed up by the sea while it was being unloaded. It represents the essence of Venice — the "Venetia" — submerged in the subconscious of its citizens. As we wend our way through Venice, we shall try to re-evoke its mystery.

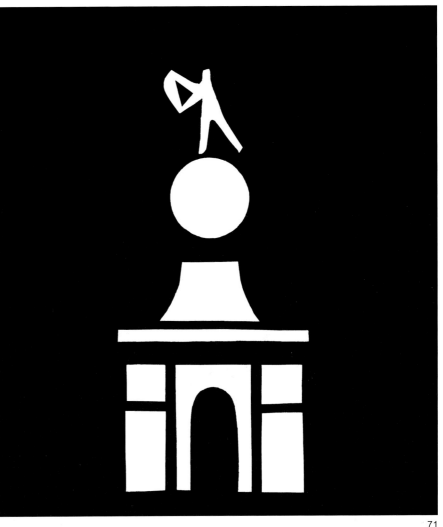

71

71. "On the sphere a bronze figure of Fortune rotates according to the direction of the wind."

THE BODY OF VENICE

The City's Inner Plan

The creative life process always follows a certain order. If we use the atomic structure of matter as an analogy, we can imagine that a city like Venice is composed of a central core around which whirls the city's dynamic organism. The core anchors the city's essential pattern, its "inner" plan, which is outwardly manifested by sanctuaries and palaces, canals and streets, houses and workshops.

To gain an insight into Venice's "inner" plan, let us start inside the Doges' Palace, which we mentioned as part of the city's core in the previous chapter. Above the Doge's throne, in the "Sala del Collegio" which we have just visited, is a painting by Paolo Veronese representing Doge Sebastiano Venier after the defeat of the Turkish fleet at Lepanto in the year 1571.

1. Palazzo Pesaro emerging out of the waters of the Grand Canal.

2. "The core anchors the city's ... 'inner plan' which is
outwardly manifested by sanctuaries and palaces ..."

The Doge and his two servants are the only live figures in the painting. Beside them stands the already dead Agostino Barbarigo, a victim of the battle, as ensign-bearer. There are also two women, one of whom personifies the city of Venice, the other the quality of Faith, and two saints, Marco and Giustina. The angels of glory and the angels of music are gathered in the clouds. The composition is completed by the image of Christ representing the Logos, his left arm embracing a glowing world sphere.

The world of the living, the world of the dead, the world of ethical values, and the world of spiritual powers are shown in dynamic interaction. There is no boundary separating the Doge and his two young servants from beings that are normally not perceived by the human eye. At the bottom of the painting, an animal resembling a lion completes the spectrum of beings belonging to the various levels of life.

3

3. *Doge Sebastiano Venier after the Defeat of the Turkish Fleet at Lepanto* by Paolo Veronese.

4. "There is no boundary separating the Doge and his two young servants from beings that are normally not perceived by the human eye."

4 ▶

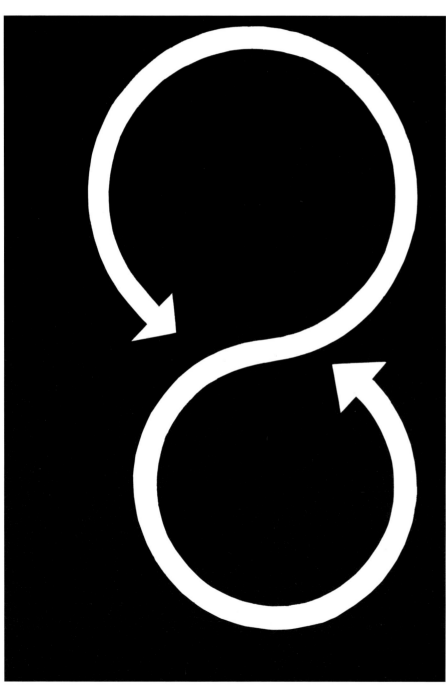

This interlacing of spiritual and physical beings is conveyed in Venice through the balanced distribution of sacred and profane buildings throughout the city's fabric. Churches and palaces — originally the homes of the aristocratic merchant families — represent the spiritual and the physical realities. Indeed it is almost impossible to find a Venetian square that is not embellished by both a church and a palace.

Together, the churches and palaces nourish the city organism with life energies that flow from two different sources. Through the sanctuaries the city absorbed spiritual energies deriving from the Cosmos. Through the commercial activities of the merchants, the physical energies of everyday life — conveyed in the form of gold, money and other material goods — flowed into the city via the family palaces. Thus the city has been "inhaling" two different substances: through its churches it has breathed in the Cosmic ether; through its palaces, the air of the Earth. If we extend the metaphor, we may almost say that the churches are one nostril of the city and the palaces the other.

5. "Together, the churches and palaces nourish the city organism with life energies that flow from two different sources."

5

6

6. Palaces and churches represent the physical and spiritual realities of the city.

The City and Its Buildings

7

Thus far we have been describing Venice's "inner" plan with respect to *space*. Yet the city grows not only in space, but also in time. With respect to *time*, the same essential pattern is apparent in the city in the co existence of various styles of art. Romanesque, Gothic, Renaissance, and Baroque buildings stand harmoniously side by side along the Grand Canal. Each of the four styles expresses a period in the city's development, a certain epoch of its spiritual and material growth.

The early centuries of the city's growth are recorded in the buildings of *Romanesque style*. Characteristic of this period is the Fondaco dei Turchi which stands by the Grand Canal. Erected in the thirteenth century for the merchant Giacomo Palmieri, it was used in the seventeenth century as a residence by the Turkish community living in Venice. In the nineteenth century its Romanesque features were completely restored.

7. The Romanesque arches of the Fondaco dei Turchi.

7

The Romanesque style is characterized by a semi-circular arch above a rectangular opening. In the universal language of art form, a rounded shape is used to represent "gentle" spirit and a rectangular shape to represent "hard" matter. The circle of the spiritual world is above, but being open toward the rectangle, it is reduced to a semi-circle. The square of the material world is below and, in turn, opens upward, extending to become a high and narrow rectangle which always has a practical function, serving as windows, doors, and corridors. There is no boundary separating the two forms. A powerful movement can be felt between them, as if a sublime fluid of spirit pours down from the arch into the hard, lifeless matter.

The Romanesque style is an expression of the youthful era of Christianity, when a feeling prevailed that spiritual power would imbue the material world and finally spiritualize the Earth. This is the period of religious inspiration and of the Crusades. The basic figure of the Romanesque style is therefore a rectangle of matter dominated by the spiritual arch.

8. "The circle of the spiritual world is above ... the square of the material world is below ..."

8

The flow of energy of the buildings erected in the *Gothic style* during the following two centuries is differently oriented. In Romanesque art the energy flows downward, while in Gothic art it flows upward. The aerodynamic shape of the pointed Gothic arch seems to pull away from the Earth, as if to lift heavy matter up to the light level of spirit. The Romanesque and Gothic styles complement each other and together give expression to the dynamics of the Middle Ages.

The succession of pointed arches on the Doges' Palace is typical of a Gothic style building. It should be experienced early in the morning when Saint Mark's Square is still bathed in tranquility: below are the arcades, above them the Loggia Foscari, and still higher, a row of windows: a graceful movement upward.

9. 'The succession of pointed arches on the Doges' Palace is typical of a Gothic-style building."

The characteristic shape of the pointed arch originates in the intersection of two circles, which results in a bi-angular form with rounded sides. We are familiar with this shape from Celtic culture which respected it as a sacred geometrical form Called the "vesica piscis" (fish bladder), it is the medial form between the circle and the triangle: no longer a circle, it has curved elements and not quite a triangle with only two angles. The circle symbolizes the unity of all life, the triangle the individuality of each particle and each being. The "vesica piscis" is thus the medial form between unity and diversity. It shows how two opposite universal qualities can manifest together without excluding each other. This symbolic content fills each pointed arch with visual power and creates a sensation of upward movement.

10

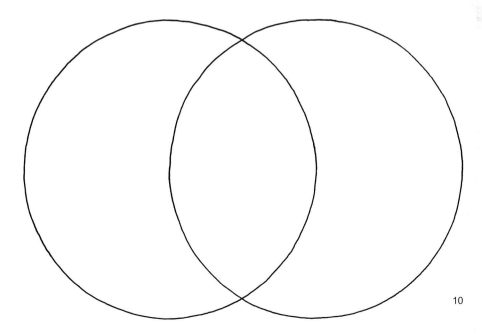

10

10. "The characteristic shape of the pointed arch originates in the intersection of two circles ..."

11

Turning one's back to the Doges' Palace, one notices yet a third style. In front of us stands the palace of the Marciana Library, designed by the architect Jacopo Sansovino in the sixteenth century. It was built in the *Renaissance style*. The edifice has three sets of horizontal lines running across the entire façade. The first set is formed by the steps leading to the arcades on the ground floor. The second set is accentuated by a richly-carved architrave supporting the first floor. The third one is formed by the balcony balustrade enclosing the roof.

Breaking these horizontals are 21 vertical lines, counterweights to gravity, whose upward movement is expressed by the hierarchy of columns. Each line has a simple Doric column at its base, a more complex Ionic column on the first floor, and a human statue at the top, in keeping with the Renaissance ideal that the human figure was the most perfect of all forms. As we can see, the lines run upward, from simple to more elaborate levels. However, if we look at the Palace as a whole, we feel no movement. The vertical and horizontal lines are in balance. Poise, order, and harmony reign in the building.

11. The palace housing the Marciana Library.

The Renaissance united and at the same time outgrew the two medieval experiences reflected in the Romanesque and Gothic styles. The balance that the Renaissance introduced is an expression of the mature period of the Christian era. This maturity enabled the Renaissance ethos to reach back toward the classical Greco-Roman culture with which it shared the same aspirations for balance and harmony. Ancient sculptures, writings and other treasures of classical culture were collected and studied, and the classical language of formal expression was re-introduced to the various branches of art.

In this way the Renaissance broadened the narrow medieval Christian concept and transformed it into a humanistic impulse valid for humanity as a whole.

12. The façade of the Marciana Library expresses the balance introduced by the Renaissance.

12

However, the growth of Venice and of European culture in general did not terminate with the emphasis on balance. The Renaissance style was followed by the *Baroque style*. At the beginning of the seventeenth century, a sense of movement reappeared in buildings. This movement tended neither downward nor upward. Instead, the buildings seem to tremble with an inner movement that spreads in all directions. In this context, let us look at the Basilica of Santa Maria della Salute, situated at the end of the Grand Canal.

The Basilica is composed of five levels. We can imagine that the inner movement starts on the ground level, lifting a portion of the roof to the next level. The inner pressure is so great that the roof stretches even further and a cupola is formed. The explosion of inner forces is still so powerful that it pierces the top of the cupola and forces out a superstructure. Even here the power of the inner movement does not cease: through the top of the superstructure it pushes the immense statue of the Virgin Mary.

When the energy reaches its apex in the statue, it descends via the cupola diagonally downward and, on the edges of the building, spirals into gigantic volutes which encircle the cupola's base.

14

14

13. The Salute Basilica expresses the movement introduced into architecture during the Baroque period.

14. Details of the Basilica of Santa Maria della Salute.

The balance between vertical and horizontal lines achieved during the Renaissance period was not forgotten in the Baroque era but developed into a dynamic kind of equilibrium. In the case of Santa Maria della Salute, the vertical movement is balanced by a horizontal movement. The pressure of the horizontal forces has created a cluster of seven chapels around the building. If one walks along the right side of the building, one can see that this violent inner explosion has caused two of the chapels almost to crash into each other.

We may say that the Baroque style is an expression of the "autumn" of both the Venetian Republic and the city itself. The Baroque buildings are as incredibly beautiful as any forest is, glowing in its colorful leafy garments, before the winter wind lays bare the branches.

15. "The pressure of the horizontal forces has created a cluster of seven chapels around the building."

15

16. "… one can see that this violent inner explosion has caused two of the chapels almost to crash into each other …"

17

17. "The Baroque buildings are as incredibly beautiful as any forest is, glowing in its colorful leafy garments, before the winter wind lays bare the branches." (Santa Maria del Giglio).

If we compare these architectural styles to seasons of the year, then Venice expresses the spring of its growth with the medieval styles of Romanesque and Gothic art (I), its summer period in the style of the Renaissance (II), and its autumn with the Baroque (III).

After the fall of the Venetian Republic in 1797, the city began to deteriorate. The creative interaction between the sacred and the profane buildings of the city was no longer understood. The sanctuaries were considered wasteful in a city where space was scarce. Of the 153 churches which once stood in the city, 35 were demolished during this period. At the same time, with the political and economic decline of the city aristocracy, many family palaces were taken over by public institutions.

In the twentieth century, however, we see a new impetus: buildings begin to be restored. This is not yet a sign of a new era, for restoration is still carried out from the "outside"; nevertheless, the crumbling is halted and healing powers begin to work within the city organism. Thus Venice stands at the threshold of a new spring, that may sprout from those elements of the old cycle can act as seed for a future cycle of growth (IV).

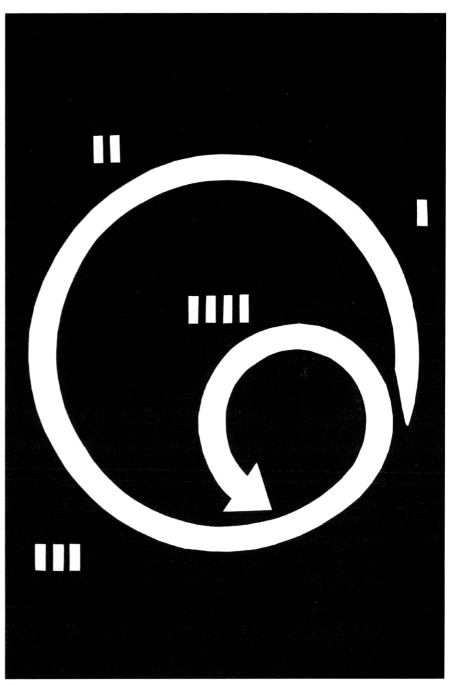

18. The four architectural styles follow the cyclic sequence of the seasons.

19. Palaces along the Grand Canal.

18

19

Saint Mark's Basilica

20

Within the body of Venice there are certain buildings which deserve more than just stylistic attention. Among them Saint Mark's Basilica has a special role to play just as the polestar does in the constellations of the night sky.

While other stars in the sky continually move, the position of the polestar remains relatively constant. To sailors on the open seas at night its position indicates the correct direction to follow. The Basilica of Saint Mark can be experienced in a similar way. Upon their arrival in Venice visitors intuitively gravitate toward the Basilica. It seems that one may enter other sanctuaries and tour the city only after having immersed oneself in Saint Mark's atmosphere in order to orientate oneself within the city as a whole.

21 ▶

20. A detail of the ceiling mosaic in Saint Mark's Basilica.

21. "While other stars in the sky continually move, the position of the polestar remains relatively constant."

22

As the "star of orientation," Saint Mark's Basilica too has remained fixed in its original form, regardless of the stylistic transformations that have taken place throughout history. All the other Venetian sanctuaries have changed according to the different periods of the city's development. Saint Mark's alone has preserved its original Romanesque structure basically unchanged throughout a millennium. Subsequent epochs have done no more than imprint their features upon its surface in the Basilica's mosaic and sculptural ornamentation.

In the lunette above the left entrance the Basilica has even preserved its "self-portrait" dating from the mid-thirteenth century. All the other mosaics on the façade were re-designed and substituted from the seventeenth to the nineteenth century. This one alone has remained untouched as the hallmark of the Basilica's temporal stability.

22. Saint Mark's Basilica is the dominant point within the city.

We have said that the "water city" has been able to maintain its identity only through adhering to the inherent pattern of the water element anchored in Saint Mark's Basilica. We have explained that the subtle energies needed for the city's growth radiate from the Golden Altar Plate inside the Basilica. These aspects of Saint Mark's are not merely a mental construct. Saint Mark's cannot be observed without our also being inwardly affected. The moment we enter the Basilica, we experience a powerful but gentle pulsation. The energies about which we talked earlier from an intellectually detached position become, in this moment, vibrant realities.

23

24

23. "In the lunette above the left entrance the Basilica has even preserved its 'self portrait'..."

24. In a detail of the sculptural ornamentation of the façade a water creature appears.

As we found during our first visit to Saint Mark's, energies of the water element pulsate in the Basilica's nave. From the Golden Altar Plate behind the high altar the energies of fire radiate toward the nave. These two different energies meet under the central cupola, where water seems to be "burnt up" by fire.

Under normal circumstances, when fire and water meet, evaporation takes place. Being heated by fire, water evaporates and ascends, leaving the heavier, impure substances behind. The result of this distillation process is pure water. The image of distillation gives us a glimpse of how the "fiery waters" of Saint Mark's work upon us.

Let us imagine ourselves entering the Basilica with a multitude of thoughts "in our head" and emotions "in our heart." In fact, these are not only confined to our head and to our heart but also form a field of energy around each one of us. Entering the whirlpool of Saint Mark's "fiery waters," the vibrations of our energy field rise — similar to the rising of the water as it evaporates — freeing us from much of the impurity that we unwittingly carry within ourselves.

25. "The image of distillation gives us a glimpse of how the 'fiery waters' of Saint Mark's work upon us."

25

When we leave the Basilica our vibrations return to their normal state just as the cooling vapor condenses back into water. But, like the distilled water, we too have been purified — by the energies of Saint Mark's Basilica.

The Basilica in its entirety can be considered a complete energy field, which is governed by the same laws as any source of electricity, requiring two poles, one negative, formed by the water energies of the nave (I), and one positive, embodied in the fire energies of the Golden Altar Plate (II). While the energy is generated at the positive pole, both poles are necessary in order to create an energy flow.

The city as a whole represents a larger energy field in which Saint Mark's acts as the positive pole (III). In order to create an energy flow, a negative pole outside the Basilica had to be built and maintained through the centuries. This pole is to be found in San Zaccaria Sanctuary (IV).

26. "In order to create an energy flow, a negative pole outside the Basilica had to be built and maintained ... (IV)."

27. A sculpture of Aquarius on the façade of Saint Mark's.

28. The vestibule of Saint Mark's Basilica.

San Zaccaria

San Zaccaria Sanctuary stands not far behind Saint Mark's Basilica. Both have been of great significance to Venice since the first years of its existence. Both were founded, in brief succession, after the seat of the young Republic had been moved from Malamocco to the islands around Rialto by the Doge Angelo Partecipazio in 810, which is considered the year of Venice's birth. San Zaccaria was founded by Angelo's successor, Giustiniano Partecipazio (827–829). In 832 the next Doge, Giovanni I Partecipazio, witnessed the consecration of the original version of Saint Mark's Basilica.

29

29. "San Zaccaria, Saint Mark's, and the settlement around Rialto were all founded in the early years of Venice's existence."

It is not surprising that San Zaccaria, Saint Mark's, and the settlement around Rialto were all founded in the early years of Venice's existence. All three are essential for the city's well-being. Currents of energy emanate from the magnetic field formed by Saint Mark's and San Zaccaria. The city centered around Rialto absorbs this energy and expresses it in the creative activity of its day-to-day life.

How is the polar relationship manifested in the two buildings?

Translated into human terms, the negative pole can be interpreted as "feminine" and the positive pole as "masculine." The feminine nature is referred to as "negative" because it creates in a passive way, facilitating life and maintaining the cycles of growth. On the other hand, the masculine nature creates in an active manner; it builds and directs, thus releasing energy of a positive charge. These two have been symbolized in different cultures by the Moon and the Sun, heavenly Mother and Father, yin and yang.

30

30. San Zaccaria Sanctuary.

31

San Zaccaria and Saint Mark's bear the signs of such a polarity in their environments. Against Saint Mark's Basilica leans the Doges' Palace, where from the early Middle Ages up to 1796 more than *one hundred men* successively led the Venetian Republic. *Innumerable other men*, members of the Council of Ten, the Senate, and the Major Council, all of which were also housed in the Doges' Palace, helped them to direct and administer Venice. Through the centuries *men alone* created, planned and worked there.

Against San Zaccaria leans the *women's cloister*, which was highly respected, as its nuns came predominantly from noble families. The convent accepted many women from families whose male members held positions of power in the Doges' Palace. These nuns spent their lives in contemplation, consecration, and tranquility.

31. The head-covering of a Doge from the Mocenigo family is carefully preserved in the Palazzo Mocenigo.

Throughout the centuries of the Venetian Republic a solemn annual ceremony was celebrated. It clarifies the symbolic relationship between Saint Mark's and San Zaccaria. Every year at Easter, the Doge and the members of the governing bodies of the Republic filed in procession from Saint Mark's to San Zaccaria where the nuns would present the Doge with a new head-covering, the token of his authority. This tradition implies that everything created and organized by the men of the Doges' Palace, however authoritative, glorious and magnificent it might have been, was ultimately of no value unless it had been sanctified by the women dedicated to the contemplative life at San Zaccaria.

32

33

32. San Zaccaria, with the women's cloister on its right, as seen from Saint Mark's Bell Tower.

33. The brick wall of the women's cloister leans against the Renaissance structure of San Zaccaria.

The positive and negative poles represented by Saint Mark's and San Zaccaria are expressed in their respective environments. The active nature of the men's creativity in the Doges' Palace affirms the positive charge associated with Saint Mark's Basilica. The passive nature of the women's service in the convent affirms the negative charge attributed to San Zaccaria.

We have said that Saint Mark's Basilica has been able to preserve its original form despite the ravages of time by generating energy from within. Its core lies beyond the dimension of space and time and is basically unaffected by the changes occurring in material reality. San Zaccaria co-operates with Saint Mark's in such a way that it grounds its energy, thus enabling the Basilica to function also within the space time dimension.

In order to do this, San Zaccaria has had to follow the stylistic transformations which have taken place in Venice throughout history. With each era of the city's development, the old San Zaccaria was abandoned and a new one arose in a form appropriate to the prevailing spirit of the times.

34

34. "Against Saint Mark's Basilica leans the Doges' Palace....
Against San Zaccaria leans the women's cloister."

35

35. A portion of the Renaissance ceiling of San Zaccaria Sanctuary.

36

Of the Romanesque aspect of San Zaccaria only the crypt is still preserved; of the Gothic structure only the former presbyterium, now known as the Chapel of San Tarasio. The Renaissance structure stands in its entirety. We would expect San Zaccaria to have been recreated once again in the Baroque manner. This, however, did not happen.

When the Renaissance period was still at its height, serious disturbances interfered with Venice's growth. The expansion of the Turkish Empire threatened the influx of material goods from the Mediterranean and the Near East. Understandably, it was the energy pole at San Zaccaria that first registered the approaching disaster, since, of all the poles of the city, it is the most sensitive to changes occurring in material reality. The energy flow between Saint Mark's and San Zaccaria was disturbed. As a result, San Zaccaria did not have sufficient impetus to effect a further change, but retained its Renaissance structure. There was to be no Baroque version of San Zaccaria.

36. Of the Gothic structure only the former presbyterium, now known as the Chapel of San Tarasio, is still preserved.

38

37

37. "Of the Romanesque aspect of San Zaccaria only the crypt is still preserved ..."

38. The Renaissance structure stands in its entirety.

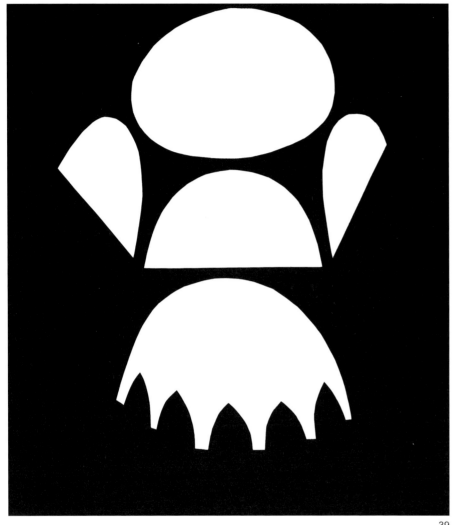

39

San Zaccaria was so closely bound up with the currents of time that even during its construction its form changed with the changing times. The construction of the present Renaissance sanctuary was started by Antonio Gambello in 1458. He began to build from the apse toward the façade, applying the Gothic arch, as the Gothic impulse was still active at that time. In 1480 he was joined by the architect Mauro Coducci. By then the Renaissance impulse had become so strong that the last Gothic elements were dropped and Coducci completed the building, including the façade, in pure Renaissance style.

39. In the choir of San Zaccaria Sanctuary we find Gothic arches combined with a Renaissance ceiling.

The façade of San Zaccaria is a perfect example of early Renaissance architecture. The central part of the façade rises above the side wings without disturbing the harmony. The architectonic structure of the façade is reflected in Giovanni Bellini's painting, dating from 1505, which radiates beauty and tranquility from an altar on the left side of the nave. On the raised throne at the center of the painting there is an image of the Virgin Mary holding her Son on her knees. She is flanked on each side by two saints, just as the wings of the façade flank its raised central part. The position in the painting corresponding to the entrance of the Sanctuary is occupied by an angel musician.

40

40. "The central part of the façade rises above the side wings without disturbing the harmony."

41

The angel's forehead and the heads of the two female saints form a perfect triangle pointing earthwards. This is the *feminine triangle*. The heads of the two men, together with the masculine head above Mary's throne, form the *masculine triangle* pointing upward. The feminine and the masculine aspects are not only differentiated but are also blended through the image of the "Great Mother" who, by the union of the masculine and the feminine forces, was able to give birth to a new life embodied in her Son.

The Son on her knees is positioned in such a way that his body constitutes a link between the "heavenly" and the "earthly" triangles. Each triangle extends upward or downward from the central point of his navel. If we imagine the masculine triangle is Saint Mark's Basilica and the feminine one the Sanctuary of San Zaccaria, the location of the Son reminds us of the close link between the two.

41. Giovanni Bellini's painting is embedded in an altar on the left side of the nave.

42. The "heavenly" and the "earthly" triangles extend upward and downward from the Child's navel.

43. *The Madonna with the Saints* by Giovanni Bellini.

San Salvador

San Salvador stands beside the city's "earth axis," which, as we discovered, runs through the "Mercerie" to the Rialto Bridge. The distance between San Salvador and Saint Mark's Basilica is approximately the same as that between Saint Mark's and San Zaccaria. San Salvador, like San Zaccaria, has a special relationship with Saint Mark's Basilica.

When we visited the Basilica of Saint Mark, we described the significance of the Golden Altar Plate. Let us underline the following: the Golden Altar Plate is not turned toward the public side of the Basilica. It turns its back to the public and faces into the intimate space behind the high altar. Its back is not bare, but clothed in a Gothic polyptych painted by Paolo Veneziano. The polyptych is the face gazing at the public, while the face of the Golden Altar Plate gazes in the opposite direction toward the realm of spiritual energies.

44

44. The relationship between San Salvador Sanctuary and Saint Mark's Basilica is reminiscent of that between the two "faces" of the Golden Altar Plate.

The Golden Altar Plate has its counterpart in the *Silver Altar Plate* (Pala d'argento) of the high altar in San Salvador Sanctuary. The form of the Silver Altar Plate evolved from the thirteenth to the fifteenth centuries and is composed of four sections, with the image of Christ's glorification in the center. Like the Golden Altar Plate, it is usually hidden from the public eye. It is covered with a painting of the same theme, the *Glorification of Christ* by Titian. Titian's painting is lowered only from August 3 to 15 and during one or two other religious holidays to reveal the Silver Altar Plate in all its splendor.

45

45. The Silver Altar Plate in San Salvador Sanctuary.

Saint Mark's Golden Altar Plate may be identified with *the positive pole*, the Sun and masculine nature. Similarly San Salvador's Silver Altar Plate would represent the complementary *negative pole*, the Moon and feminine nature. The silvery light of the Moon and the golden light of the Sun are symbols of the two basic creative forces and in Venice these are manifested in the Silver and the Golden Altar Plates.

46. In Venice the two basic creative forces are manifested in the Golden and Silver Altar plates.

Both San Salvador and San Zaccaria have their own special relationship to Saint Mark's Basilica. They also have a particular relationship to each other. Like San Zaccaria, San Salvador is an old sanctuary; it too has changed with the changing times and, like San Zaccaria, it has preserved its Renaissance structure.

But San Salvador must be more deeply involved with material reality, for it has advanced further in the cycles of the city's growth than San Zaccaria. We no longer find elements of the Gothic style in its construction as we do in San Zaccaria. San Salvador was built in the purest Renaissance style and even went beyond the horizon of the Renaissance with its Baroque façade.

47

47. "San Salvador ... even went beyond the horizon of the Renaissance with its Baroque façade."

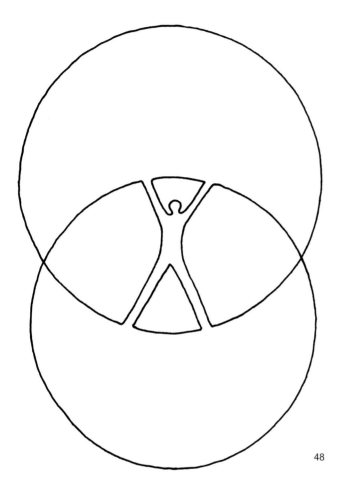

48

The Sanctuary is not normally entered from the façade, but through the side entrance from the main commercial streets, the "Mercerie." It seems that San Salvador channels the precious energies generated by Saint Mark's Basilica into the densest material spheres of Venice's life: the life that revolves around material goods and money. It is understandable therefore that the theme of transfiguration — the process whereby matter is transmuted into light — is strongly evoked in this Sanctuary. This is the central motif of the "Glorification of Christ," depicted on both the Silver Altar Plate and the painting by Titian that covers it.

48. In the transfiguration theme, the human being is the link between matter, the lower circle, and light, the upper circle.

The architectural language of the building is also in keeping with this theme. Three identical cupolas rise in a row above the nave. Their arches glitter in dazzling light, which enters through apertures above, opened with great care in 1574 by the architect Scamozzi. This light is one of the essential elements of the Sanctuary.

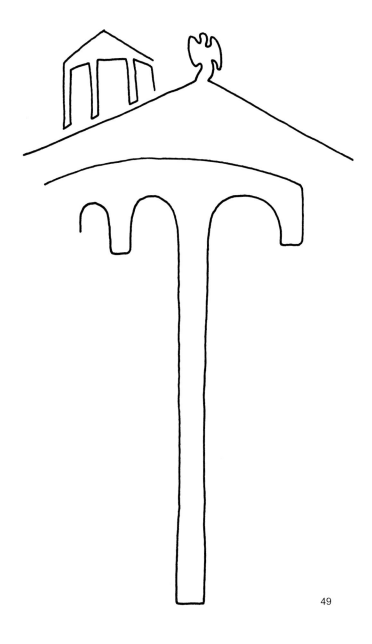

49

49. On the roof of san Salvador Sanctuary we can see the apertures created by the architect Scamozzi.

50

The ground plan of each cupola is outlined below on the Sanctuary floor in the form of a circular pattern of multi-colored marble. As we walk across each ground plan, these same circular patterns are sublimated in the light of the cupolas high above. What we see on the ground at the material level as hard, angular, stony patterns, we perceive above us as a soft, intangible mist of light within the cupola's vault.

The architecture of San Salvador evokes a mental response to the process whereby matter is sublimated into light. This mental response is articulated gradually as we walk from the first cupola to the second, and from the second to the third, step by step, similar to the way in which we form a sentence, word by word.

Although San Salvador and San Zaccaria both ground the energy of Saint Mark's Basilica, their roles are different. This diversity can be seen in two paintings, both by Giovanni Bellini, one commissioned for San Zaccaria, the other for San Salvador.

50. "Three identical cupolas rise in a row above the nave."

51. "The ground plan of each cupola is outlined below on the Sanctuary floor ..."

51

In San Salvador, to the left of the high altar, hangs the painting *Supper at Emmaus*. Supper is part of the "routine" of life as it is conditioned by matter. We are not, however, looking at an everyday supper. The painting is filled with peace and concentration, transmuting the usual meal into a rite.

The light falling from the left illuminates Christ's head, the seat of consciousness. His consciousness transforms the light into the blessing expressed in the gesture of his right hand. The power of blessing is then transferred to the bread he is holding in his left hand. The absolute light from above has been brought down to the level of daily bread.

The transfiguration theme is here complemented by the theme of manifestation: the process whereby light is gradually transmuted into matter. Thus the cosmic cycle of matter and light is completed.

◀ 52

53

54

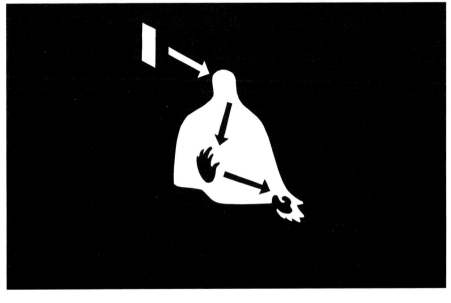

52. "As we walk across each ground plan, these same circular patterns are sublimated in the light of the cupolas high above."

53. The *Supper at Emmaus* by Giovanni Bellini.

54. The light falling from the left is transferred to the bread Christ is holding.

55

55. The feminine and the masculine qualities are universal and inherent within every human being.

The scene of the meal contains five male figures and, even though no female figure is present, the painting does evoke a feminine quality: the ability to radiate love, peace and beauty through material reality. Here we must clarify that the feminine qualities do not belong solely to women, nor do the masculine qualities belong strictly to men. Both qualities are universal and are inherent in each woman and each man.

In San Zaccaria, when explaining Bellini's painting, we emphasized one of the feminine qualities: the ability to create a flow of life, generation after generation, as a result of the union of opposite forces. San Salvador highlights another of the feminine qualities: the ability to sustain light within the concrete forms of daily life.

56

56. San Salvador Sanctuary presses tightly against the adjoining houses.

Salute

57

The Basilica of Santa Maria della Salute, referred to as Salute, was conceived as a gesture of gratitude for liberation from the plague that raged through the city in 1630. It was erected by the architect Baldassare Longhena between the years 1631 and 1681.

The idea of building Salute sprang up, so to speak, in a moment, as the city's emotional reaction to the deadly effects of the plague. Its architectural structure thus has no prehistory. Everything in the Basilica belongs to the same moment in time. Even today, Salute preserves the same image as it had at the moment of its eruptive formation.

57. "... Salute sprang up ... in a moment, as the city's emotional reaction ..."

58. The Basilica of Santa Maria della Salute.

58

Sailing past Salute on the Grand Canal provides an ever changing perspective of the Basilica from which we can see how its exuberant baroque form accords with its emotional origin. It seems that the Basilica exists only because the "emotional reaction" is exploding in its interior again and again. No mental concept alone would be strong enough to maintain the tension of the numerous protuberances of the Basilica's structure.

59

60

59. "No mental concept alone would be strong enough to maintain the tension of the numerous protuberances..."

60. Interlaced swastikas, originally a symbol of the sun-wheel, on the façade of Salute Basilica.

If we speak of Salute as an emotional creation, we must underline two things. First of all, emotionality should not be identified as something transitory, superficial and therefore inferior. Although a feeling exists only at a given moment, it permeates one's whole being. This all embracing quality of the emotions accumulates inwardly and eventually blooms as wisdom. In contrast to mental constructs, which have a masculine quality, wisdom, based upon simple being and sensitivity, is a distinctly feminine quality.

As though to confirm Salute's dedication to timeless wisdom, two sacred and ancient ornaments circle it: outside, sequences of interlaced swastikas — originally a symbol of the sun-wheel — and inside, a band of spirals.

61

61. "As though to confirm Salute's dedication to timeless wisdom, two sacred and ancient ornaments circle it ..."

Entering Salute and looking toward the center of the Basilica's paving, we see a small, circular metal plate. This plate marks the locus of the central axis around which Salute "revolves." All the Basilica's elements are symmetrically arranged around this invisible axis, evoking a sensation of circular movement. Our planet Earth also has such an axis around which it revolves in cosmic space. Ancient traditions speak of an invisible axis around which the whole of life is spinning. It is called "the axis of the world" (axis mundi). Shall we imagine that Santa Maria della Salute is spinning around the "axis mundi"?

62

62. The metal plate within the wreath of roses in the center of the pavement marks the locus of the axis around which Salute revolves.

Three spaces, hierarchically superimposed one above the other, circle the axis. The lowest space is reserved for the physical being of humans. The space above opens into a cupola and is encircled by a balcony, a symbol for the presence of beings to whom the law of gravity does not apply. These beings, whose substance is similar to our thoughts and feelings, are called spiritual beings. But we must emphasize that we ourselves are also partly spiritual beings, capable of rising to this spiritual realm despite the physical nature of our bodies, as happens at the moment of death or when, contemplating the nature of the world, our thoughts and feelings rise upward.

63

63. "Three spaces, hierarchically superimposed one above the other, circle the axis."

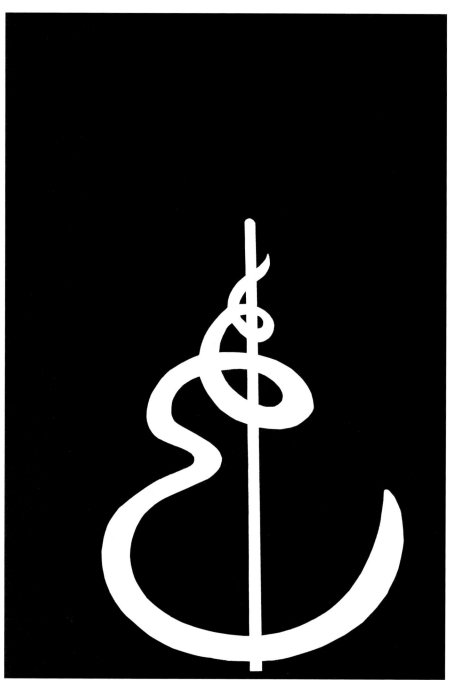

The highest space inside the Basilica is the cupola's superstructure. This space is so narrow that it seems we can reach it neither with our thoughts nor our feelings, and least of all with our bodies. Indeed, it is intended neither for human nor for other beings but is rather the realm of the Logos, the universal principle that governs the whole spectrum of life pulsating in the spaces beneath. This highest space is permeated with something indescribable. It is for this very reason that it was built in such a way that we can scarcely discern its internal arrangement.

64

64. The Basilica's elements are arranged around the invisible axis, suggesting circular movement.

65. "The highest space inside the Basilica ... is the realm
of the Logos, the universal principle ..."

66

From this highest point a reverse momentum in the Basilica's energy flow unexpectedly occurs. That which is most hidden and least attainable descends directly within human reach in the form of a sumptuous lantern. The lantern hangs from the conflux of three iron supports that block the entrance to the cupola's superstructure. The conflux is set precisely at the center of the superstructure so that the lantern descends along the Basilica's invisible axis. Its lowest part and the small brass plate on the ground, marking the locus of the axis, gaze at each other "eye to eye." In poetic terms we might say that the highest principle of the Cosmos is present also in every human heart as its "internal lantern."

67

66. Along the Basilica's vertical axis the lantern cable descends from the cupola's superstructure.

67. Looking upward along the Basilica's axis, we see the perfect alignment of the lantern directly above our heads with the cupola far above.

As embodied in Salute, the hierarchy of life not only ascends in three successive stages to its highest point; in its fourth stage it begins its descent, to return, in its fifth and final stage, to its point of departure on the ground. Rather than talking in terms of hierarchy, we should speak in terms of the universal cycle of life.

68 ▶

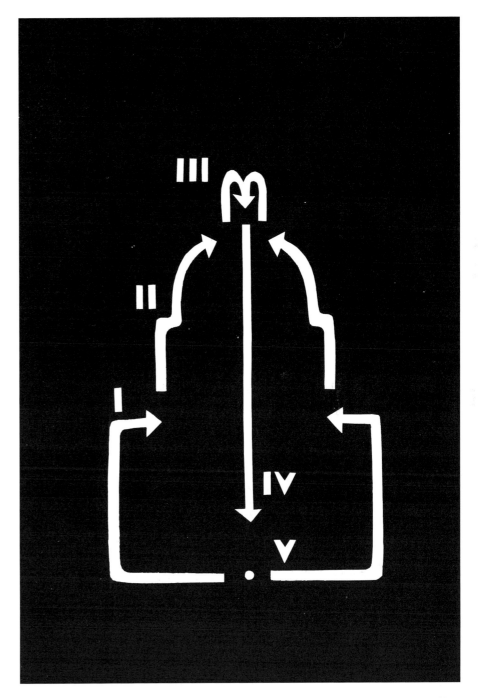

68. "As embodied in Salute the hierarchy of life not only ascends in three successive stages to its highest point; in its fourth stage it begins its descent ..."

Each of the Basilica's five spaces has its own source of light. The lower space receives its light through the windows and doors; the cupola through the circle of apertures at its base. The source of the thick, milky-white light illuminating the superstructure is virtually hidden from our view. There is a gradation in the intensity of light in the upward direction, the light at the top being the brightest. The source of the fourth light is the lantern glowing at the Basilica's axis immediately above our heads, and the glow of the Basilica's polished paving is the source of the fifth light. Downward-moving light hits the polished surface of the paving and "pushes away" from the ground in a vertical direction. Thus a symbolic circulation of light is formed in the Basilica: from cosmic sources light descends to the Earth and the reflection of our creativity shines back toward the Cosmos.

◀ 69

69. Light from the superstructure of the Basilica reappears on the earthly level as the light of the lantern and finally reflects in the glow of the polished paving.

We have been imagining Santa Maria della Salute spinning around the "axis of the world." This circular movement is expressed on the horizontal plane, first of all, in the Basilica's paving, which is composed of several concentric bands of multi-colored marble. The round metal plate in the middle, "the locus of the Basilica's axis," now reveals an additional meaning.

If we consider the metal plate in the center of the floor as the "navel of the universe," Salute becomes complete as a microcosm. The horizontal motion starting concentrically from the navel — the point of our original link with the mother — corresponds to the maternal creation in the universe, the cosmic Mother. The hierarchy of life spiraling around the vertical axis represents the paternal creation, the cosmic Father. Both directions of creation are united, mystically, in the small metal plate adorned with a wreath of colored marble roses. The wreath is the first of the concentric bands composing the Basilica's paving.

70

70. The horizontal movement expressed by the Basilica's ground plan is drawn upward by the energy of its vertical axis to form a spiral dance.

The designs of each subsequent band on the paving become more and more geometric in form. Finally, at its outermost circumference, this concentric movement spirals upward to be molded into eight triumphal arches encircling the Basilica's ground level. The first serves as the entrance into the Basilica, the other seven open into chapels. Each chapel has equal access to the central space of the Basilica.

If we interpret the Basilica's ground plan symbolically, we would say that from the "navel of the universe" several patterns of wisdom unfold: each of the seven chapels corresponds to a system of spiritual cognition.

71

72 ▶

71. The concentric bands of the Basilica's paving spread out beneath the lantern.

72. From the "navel of the universe" the Basilica's ground plan gradually unfolds through eight triumphal arches into the side chapels.

73

At the time when Salute was erected, the dominant system of cognition in Europe was Christianity. The chapel corresponding to this era was therefore expanded into an autonomous "minor" sanctuary where the high altar is located.

Between the "major" sanctuary and the "minor" one there is a relationship similar to that between Saint Mark's Basilica and the Doges' Palace. One is an expression of the eternal dimension of life, the other of the particular epoch during which the building flourished.

The "major" sanctuary of Salute, as a sanctuary of universal wisdom, stands outside the bounds of time. The "minor" sanctuary, however, is bound to the two millennia dominated by the bi-polar sign of Pisces. Just as the complex of the Doges' Palace is split into two halves — the palace and the jails — so the cupola of the "minor" sanctuary is split into two half-cupolas. The palace and the jails are linked by the Bridge of Sighs. Likewise, both halves of the cupola in the "minor" sanctuary of Salute are linked by the base of a second cupola which vaults above them.

73. The cupola of the "minor" sanctuary is split into two half-cupolas linked by a second cupola centered above them.

74

74

74. "The 'minor' sanctuary... is bound to the two millenia dominated by the bi-polar sign of Pisces."

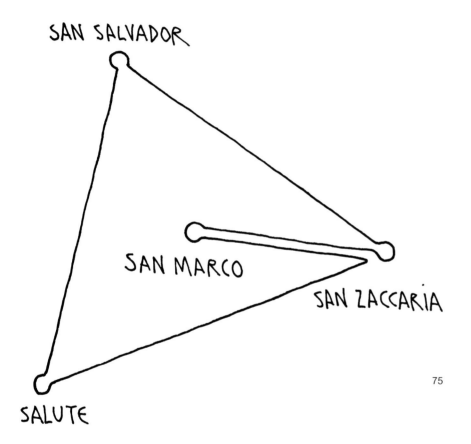

SAN SALVADOR

SAN MARCO

SAN ZACCARIA

SALUTE

Santa Maria della Salute is a sanctuary of wisdom. To embed this quality in the city fabric, Salute had to be erected at the end of the Grand Canal, where it could become part of the city core. To place the Basilica at the correct spot, the Venetians had to sacrifice the Church of the Holy Trinity, which had stood there for a long time.

However, in this substitution another trinity was created: three sanctuaries embodying the feminine qualities — San Zaccaria, San Salvador, and Salute — form a triangle around Saint Mark's Basilica.

75

75. Three sanctuaries embodying the feminine qualities form a triangle around Saint Mark's Basilica.

76. The cupolas of Santa Maria della Salute, a sanctuary dedicated to wisdom, rise above the end of the Grand Canal.

San Sebastiano

77

Whereas we recognized Saint Mark's as having an affinity with the water element and Salute with emotional expression, San Sebastiano could be said to have an affinity with music.

When listening to music, we are bathed in currents of sound. The music emerging from its source whirls around us and finally flows away into silence. One and the same space contains the source of the music, the plenitude of its presence, and its end in silence.

Let us imagine that while music is being played, every tone and musical phrase "petrifies" into matter. San Sebastiano's ambience embodies this process. When we stand in San Sebastiano, it is as though we were standing in the midst of music made matter. Musical phrases normally come and go; in San Sebastiano they are caught, halted in their flow and transformed into color and form. In our first moment in San Sebastiano we feel somewhat uncomfortable, for we are meeting in static form something we are used to encountering in motion.

In order to transform music into matter, two conditions had to be met. First of all, the architect had to minimize the symbolic content of the architectural language. In Santa Maria della Salute it is possible to distinguish the meaning of any element and its significance for the building as a whole. San Sebastiano, however, seems empty and dull in this respect. Its primary aim is to speak with the language of music, not with the language of architecture. The architect's task was merely to prepare an appropriate vessel for this musical flow. The building, built between 1505 and 1548 by the architect Lo Scarpagnino, is distinguished by its harmonious proportions and simplicity of construction.

77. San Sebastiano Sanctuary.

78. "The building ... is distinguished by its harmonious proportions and simplicity of construction."

79. The organ, suspended from the left wall, dominates the interior of San Sebastiano Sanctuary.

The second condition that had to be met was that someone would dedicate his life to the task of attuning himself repeatedly to the music which "plays" here, for music occurs in time, and it could materialize rhythmically only over a lengthy period.

This condition was met by Paolo Caliari of Verona, the painter better known as Paolo Veronese. In 1555 his compatriot, the Abbot of the monastery that stood beside San Sebastiano, invited him to paint the ceiling of the sacristy in San Sebastiano. This was Veronese's first work of art executed in Venice, initiating his career as a Venetian painter. In the musical context we have been considering, the ceiling of the sacristy represents the overture.

80

81

80. Detail of the Sanctuary's ceiling with a scene from the life of Queen Esther.

81. Veronese's portrait can be seen at the side of the organ.

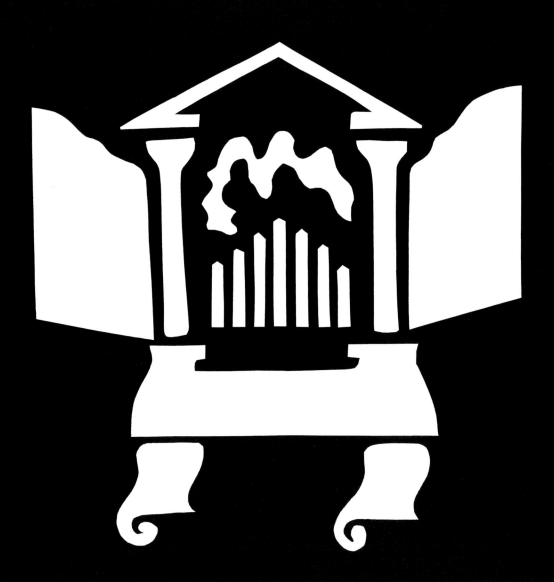

During the next year, Veronese painted the Sanctuary ceiling with scenes from the life of Queen Esther. In the following years, he frescoed the walls. In 1561 he completed the painting for the high altar and afterward the two large paintings at the sides. Some parts of the presbyterium ceiling remained blank — as they are still today — because in 1588 Veronese's life cycle came to an end. The fact that no other artist completed the painting of the ceiling is a further indication of the unique relationship that Veronese had with the sanctuary. His tomb and that of his brother were placed to the left of the high altar below the famous organ, which Veronese himself had designed and painted. His portrait, of seventeenth-century date, can be seen at the side of the organ.

The organ projects into the Sanctuary from the wall to the left of the high altar. Veronese painted both sides of the organ door and shaped its entire form. The organ is so beautiful and prominent that it outshines even the visual power of the high altar. It is the central object in San Sebastiano and proclaims the dominant role of musical creation in the Sanctuary.

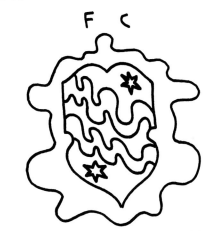

83

◀ 82

82. "The organ ... proclaims the dominant role of musical creation in the Sanctuary."

83. The inscriptions on Veronese's tombstone.

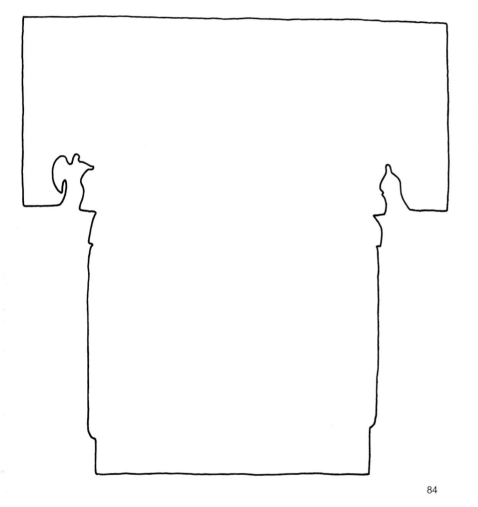

84

To make contact with the music in its material form, let us look at the fresco of the Annunciation on the triumphal arch above the high altar. To the left of the arch is the Angel speaking the words of the Annunciation to Mary who is listening from the other side. In the middle of the nave the motif of the Annunciation is repeated in the form of two sculptures. In one corner of the choir the statue of the Angel stands "talking" across the Sanctuary to Mary, who is "listening" from the opposite corner. Such a repetition of the same scene is meaningful only as a musical theme which is repeated again and again with variations.

84. "In one corner of the choir the statue of the Archangel stands 'talking' across the Sanctuary to Mary, who is 'listening' from the opposite corner."

Another example of musical treatment can be seen in the fresco depicting the death of Saint Sebastian. The fresco occupies both sides of the Sanctuary. On the left the soldiers loose their arrows, which fly invisibly across the Sanctuary and strike Saint Sebastian's body on the other side. If we imagine that the soldiers personify a musical instrument, each arrow flying off a bow represents a musical tone leaving the instrument. Saint Sebastian, on the opposite side of the Sanctuary, personifies silence, for the arrows come to a standstill in his body. In the same way, musical tones, like arrows, pierce the air and strike the listener's ear before fading into silence.

85 ▶

85. "If we imagine that the soldiers personify a musical instrument, each arrow flying off a bow represent a musical tone …"

San Sebastiano's musical content is its outwardly-directed level of expression. What then is San Sebastiano's inner essence? We begin to feel it when we look upward to the Sanctuary's marvelous ceiling. The three central canvases were painted by Veronese in such a way that they radiate a quality as clear as spring water. Let us imagine a spring seen in nature: a jet of cool water bursting from the unknown depths of the Earth and cascading over a stone.

When we look at the canvas nearest the high altar, we should keep the above image in mind. Mordecai has saved the life of the Assyrian King and is now in triumphal march through the streets of the capital. The painting is conceived in such a way that horses, servants and Mordecai himself seem to be marching directly upon us, evoking the image of water bursting out of a spring. This "water," however, is not flowing out of the Earth, but out of the depths of the firmament.

86. *Triumphal March* by Paolo Veronese, from the Sanctuary's ceiling.

We may well ask what kind of energy springs from the depths of the universe and uses our bodies as its channel. This energy, which pulsates throughout the universe and keeps all beings alive, is called by us "life energy." The ancient Greeks knew it as "etheric energy" and the Hindus as "prana." Like any living organism, a city can also live, grow and develop only as long as a field of this life energy pulsates through it.

It is not by chance that in San Sebastiano we have become aware of this field of life energy pulsating through Venice. The sensitive musical ambience of San Sebastiano is an appropriate medium for the manifestation of this subtle energy field. San Sebastiano constitutes together with the Basilica Santa Maria della Salute and Saint Mark's Basilica another trinity among the Venetian sanctuaries. They are positioned on a slightly bent line that follows the edge of the city along the Giudecca Canal. The energies of Saint Mark's Basilica as the city's "focus of identity" and of Salute as the "temple of wisdom" unite with the "life energy source" in San Sebastiano Sanctuary to work upon the whole organism of Venice.

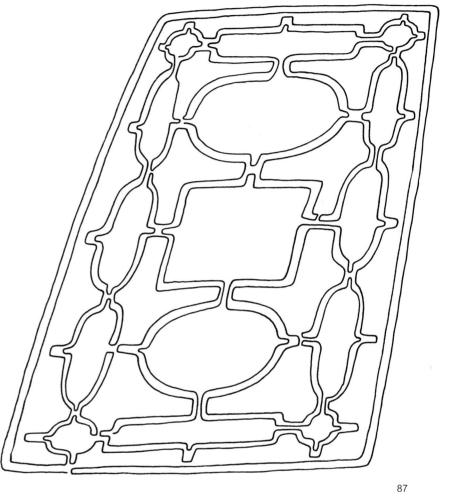

87

87. The pattern on the Sanctuary's ceiling is analogous to the designs created by vibrating energy fields.

San Pietro di Castello

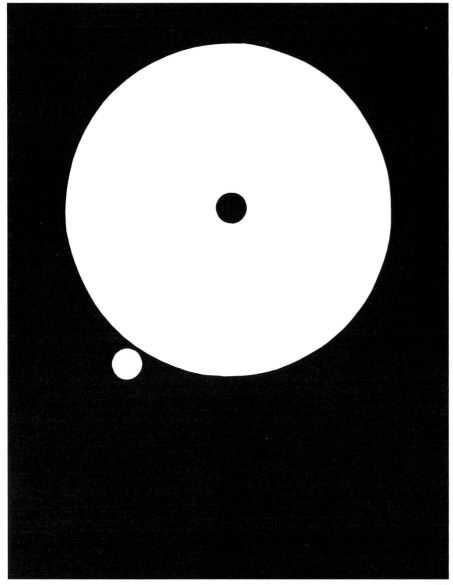

Apart from the polestar, Polaris, which we have mentioned in connection with Saint Mark's Basilica, there is another star of great interest to us in the night sky — Sirius. It outshines every other star and has been observed for millennia. Seen in the northern hemisphere, it traces a characteristic path that curves low across the edge of the nocturnal firmament.

In Venice the church of greatest interest to us from a historical point of view also lies at the edge of the city. San Pietro di Castello, the former *Cathedral of Venice*, lies at the most distant point of the city on the islet of Olivolo. From 775 onwards this was the institutional seat of Venice's spiritual power and remained so until 1807, when Napoleon decreed that this role should henceforth be filled by Saint Mark's Basilica.

88. "Sirius ... traces a characteristic path that curves low across the edge of the nocturnal firmament."

88

For a thousand years the official spiritual center
in San Pietro and the political center in the
Doges' Palace maintained a balance of power in
Venice. The location of each center within the
city structure is noteworthy. The political power
of the Doges' Palace operated within the flow of
time, and it was therefore located *in the city center*.
The spiritual power of San Pietro, on the other
hand, operated in silence and tranquility outside
the flow of time. Venice's cathedral therefore
stands on the edge of the city.

Cathedrals are normally found in the center of
cities. Venice, however, placed its own cathedral
on the city's outskirts. This exceptional decision
was made because Venice had for millennia been
developing unique approaches to spirituality.
In this context the frequent confrontations
between the Pope in Rome and the Venetian
Republic are significant. The culmination of
these disputes was reached in 1606 when Venice
was excommunicated for about a year from the
Church.

89 ▶

89. The former Cathedral of Venice lies at the most distant
point of the city on the islet of Olivolo.

90

The special relationship of Venice with spirituality becomes clear when we consider the role of Saint Mark's Basilica in the balance of power between the Doges' Palace and the Cathedral of San Pietro.

Although the Doge was the *political leader* of Venice with his seat in the Doges' Palace, the fact that Saint Mark's was called "the Doge's private Basilica" indicates that he also assumed a kind of *spiritual leadership* within Venice. The Cathedral of San Pietro on the other hand was the city's *public cathedral*. We have therefore not only two centers of power but three: in the city center the Doges' Palace and Saint Mark's Basilica, and on the outskirts of the city, the Cathedral of San Pietro.

90. The bell tower of San Pietro di Castello.

The triangular relationship of these three buildings is reminiscent of the tripartite system of ancient Egypt: the Pharaoh as ruler, the Pharaoh as the high priest, and the official priesthood. The Pharaoh as ruler would correspond in Venice to the Doge's Palace, and the Pharaoh as the high priest to the Doge's Basilica of Saint Mark. Both buildings stand side by side, strictly separated yet linked by a secret passage. The Egyptian priesthood would be equivalent to the role played throughout the centuries by the Cathedral of San Pietro di Castello.

91

91. The triangular relationship of Saint Mark's Basilica (I), the Doges' Palace (II), and the Cathedral of San Pietro di Castello (III).

92

92. Details of the façade of San Pietro di Castello.

92

93

By virtue of San Pietro's position in the city structure we have noticed a link with Sirius; by virtue of San Pietro's role in Venice's leadership we have also discovered a link with ancient Egypt. San Pietro, however, although covered in external splendor, has been robbed of its ancient honors, and thus reveals nothing of its deeper nature to the casual visitor.

We can sense San Pietro's hidden dimension in two places. One is to be found inside the Cathedral to the left of the high altar in the Vendramin Chapel. The Chapel was created by Baldassarre Longhena, the architect whose work we know from the Salute Basilica. Twelve marble figures adorning the sides of the Chapel personify through their gestures and the objects they hold or touch distinct qualities of universal life.

94

93. San Pietro di Castello, at the edge of the city, as seen from Saint Mark's Bell Tower.

94. San Pietro di Castello is separated from the passing canal by a small park.

The most interesting from our point of view are the two female figures standing on each side of the entrance. They radiate supreme beauty. Both remind us of the relationship to the stars we have intuited in connection with San Pietro. The figure on the left bears on her breast the image of our parent star, the Sun. She is touching a sphere with her foot, presumably the Earth. She represents the Logos of our solar system. The figure on the right bears three six-pointed stars and is holding a hollow "sphere" denoting the larger sphere of our galaxy within which our solar system is located. She could be related to Sirius, traditionally the home of our galactic Logos.

95. "The figure... bears on her breast the image of our parent star, the Sun."

95

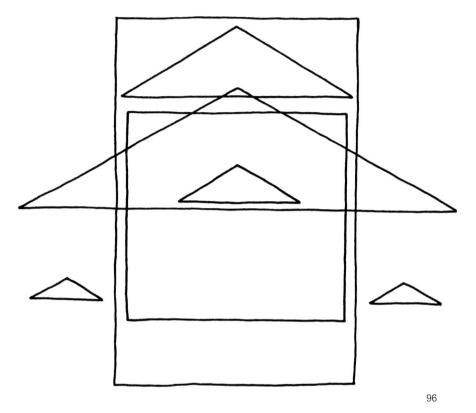

96

The second place from which we can sense the deeper nature of San Pietro is in the park outside the Cathedral. Around us we see the former Patriarch's Palace, the sloping Renaissance belfry, and San Pietro's façade. Here, in the stillness, one can pick up vibrations that can be felt nowhere else in the city.

Diagonally across the park runs a stone path leading to the façade. If we approach San Pietro on this path, we have a sensation of walking on one side of a triangle. Looking up at the façade (previously hidden by trees), we catch sight of five triangles, sharply drawn in stone. The basic harmony of the façade is achieved through three triangles, one above each of the three doors. Above these a fourth triangle extends. The fifth one is almost invisible; we notice only its two angles above the side naves.

96. The triangles and rectangles of the façade of San Pietro di Castello.

In addition to these five triangles, two rectangles are also drawn on the façade of San Pietro. The first marks the central field of the façade and includes the main entrance. The second rectangle encloses the first, as well as the large triangle above, and marks the horizontal top of the façade.

Two other basilicas with façades composed of triangles and rectangles stand on the edge of the city. They are San Giorgio Maggiore on the islet of San Giorgio and the Redentore on the islet of Giudecca.

All three basilicas were constructed by Andrea Palladio, the Renaissance architect and poet. In 1558 he began work first on the Basilica of San Pietro, which was later completed by his successors. Palladio, as we know, was well versed in the geometry of Pythagoras, the great Greek philosopher who related his geometry to the length of sound waves. By altering the length of a string or a pipe, we alter the sound produced.

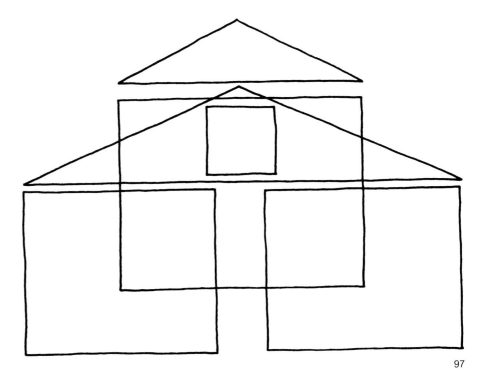

97

97. The composition of the façade of the Basilica of San Giorgio Maggiore.

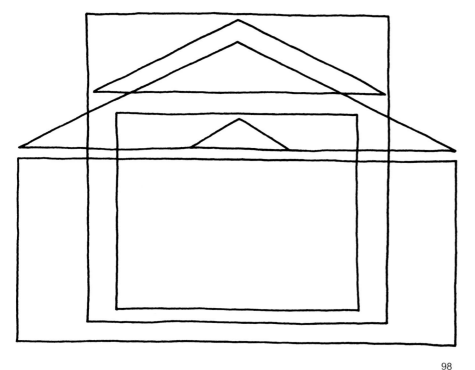

98

We can now see Palladio's use of triangles and rectangles in a new light. The three vertices of a triangle and the four corners of a rectangle jointly represent the seven notes in the diatonic scale. The distances between these points can be thought of as the seven basic intervals in music. Consequently we can consider the façades of Palladio's basilicas as sound compositions!

If we take a closer look at the three façades, we shall discover that the triangles and rectangles on each one are arranged quite differently. Their number also differs. We can therefore presume that each façade vibrates to a different tune. Could it also be that the sound composition of each façade finds its complement in the vibrations resonating in the corresponding interior of the three basilicas?

98. The composition of the façade of the Redentore Basilica.

99. Coming along the diagonal path through the park toward San Pietro di Castello, we walk on one side of a triangle.

99

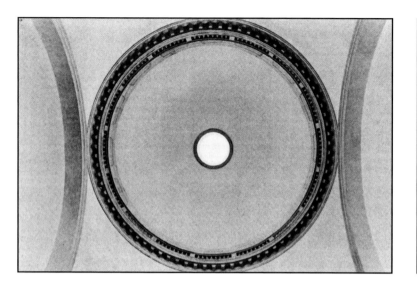

100

100. Do the vibrations of the interior of San Pietro di Castello complement the sound composition of its façade?

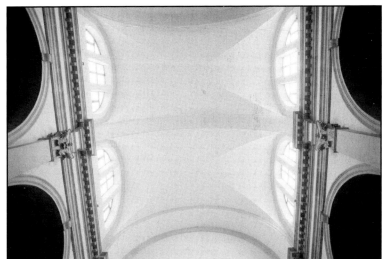

100

San Giorgio Maggiore

101

Palladio's architecture based on sound composition can be experienced most fully in San Giorgio Maggiore. The Basilica stands in the grounds of an ancient monastery on the islet bearing the same name. Although it was erected on the other side of Saint Mark's Basin, it nevertheless contributes with the triangles and rectangles of its façade to the dignity of the area around Saint Mark's.

On entering the Basilica, we are almost disappointed by its elevated emptiness. But this is only an impression imparted by the Basilica's physical structure. San Giorgio Maggiore becomes beautiful if we relax and "listen" carefully to the interweaving of vibrations which resonate in the Basilica and through it into the atmosphere of Venice.

The extraordinary features of San Giorgio Maggiore and its two sister basilicas, San Pietro and the Redentore, are the "sound" vibrations that resonate within them.

101. The Basilica of San Giorgio Maggiore.

We have explained the musical nature of the compositions of the façades. But the vibrations present in their interiors are not derived from the composition of triangles and rectangles, as on the façades, but from the two- and three-dimensional relationships between the various architectonic elements.

Here we are not thinking of the formal relationships created by architectonic masses (for example by the Basilica's length and width), but rather of the energy that flows between two architectonic forms, just as it flows between two stones, or two people. Relationship is in fact an invisible and physically unmeasurable energetic tension, but is not, for that reason, any less real than physical matter.

It may be hard to imagine that sounds, which are audible, have a direct link to architecture, which is silent. Yet there are relationships between the separate notes in a musical composition that can be thought of as energy tensions between sounds. These are known in musical theory as the intervals — the first, the second, the third, etc. They are similar to the relationships existing between different architectonic forms.

102. A characteristic energy flow may be felt between the curved arches and the angular architraves within San Giorgio Maggiore.

103

103. The architectural rhythms of San Giorgio Maggiore's façade.

103

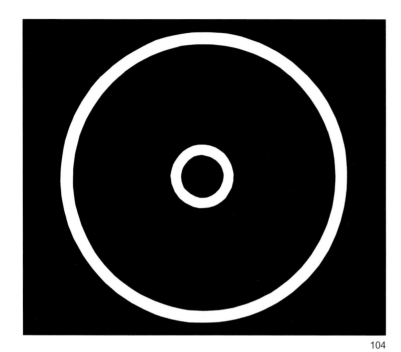

104

105

Each interval gives a particular quality to the sounds that it separates. To make a distinction between this quality and the sound of musical notes themselves, we shall call it "the inner sound." It can be perceived only intuitively as energy tension. So too with the relationship between architectonic forms.

Where in the Basilica do the "musical," i.e. architectural intervals sound? In the interiors of Palladio's basilicas we can intuit the first interval in the relationship between equally-shaped two-dimensional forms. For example, if we stand at the center of the Basilica below the cupola and look straight up, we shall see the cupola's perimeter and high above it the smaller perimeter of the cupola's superstructure. Between these two circles the first interval resonates.

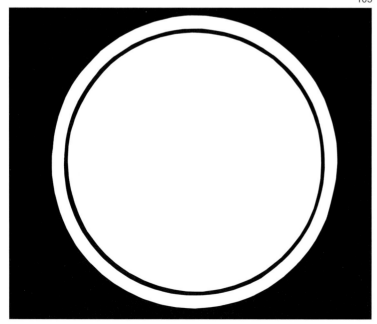

104. "We can intuit the first interval in the relationship between the cupola's perimeter and the smaller perimeter of the cupola's superstructure."

105. The second interval ... will be perceived in the relationship between the cupola's perimeter and the imaginary plane that the perimeter encloses.

The second interval is equivalent to the relationship between an architectonic element and its complement. If we look upward again, the second interval will be perceived in the relationship between the cupola's perimeter and the imaginary plane that the perimeter encloses.

The third interval consists in the relationship between an element and its supplement. For example, the cupola's base is demarcated by a cornice that follows an angular path, while higher up another cornice circles the cupola in a curved path. Between these two cornices we can "hear" the third interval.

The fourth interval denotes a relationship between elements that play an equivalent role in the building without necessarily having similar shapes. In the Basilica the fourth interval sounds between the balcony that adorns the perimeter of the cupola and the ornamentation on the perimeter of the superstructure.

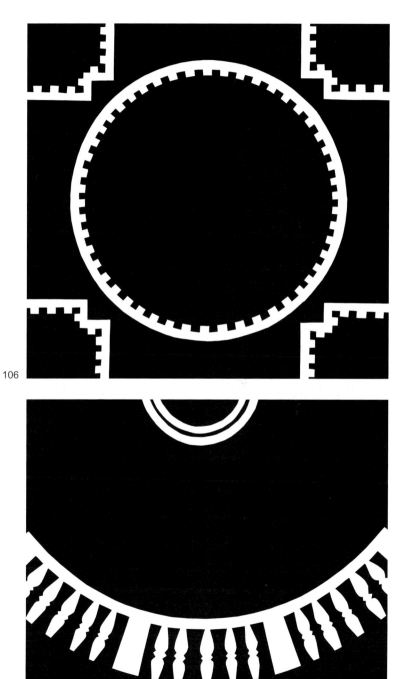

106

107

106. The third interval may be "heard" in the relationship between the cornice on the cupola's base, which follows an angular path, and the cornice on its perimeter, which forms a circular path.

107. "The fourth interval sounds between the balcony that adorns the perimeter of the cupola and the ornamentation on the perimeter of the superstructure."

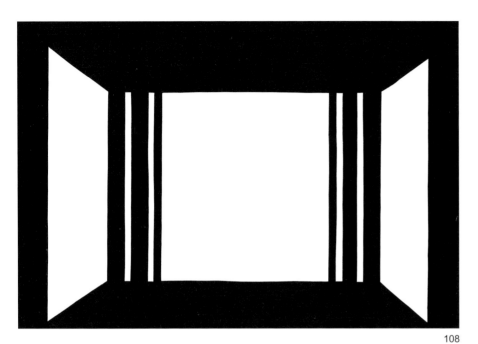

The fifth can be found in the relationship between architectonic elements with opposite roles in the building. In San Giorgio, a fifth interval reverberates between the vertical lines of the composite pillars supporting the cupola and the empty three-dimensional space they embrace.

The sixth interval is expressed in the relationship between elements of a two-dimensional and those of a three-dimensional nature. For example, the cupola rests above a square ground plan that gives way to the rounded space within the four vaults. The sixth interval sounds in the relationship between the square of the floor and the rounded space created by the vaults.

With the seventh interval we denote the relationship between two three-dimensional elements. In San Giorgio, an example of the seventh can be found in the Basilica's main nave. The seventh interval resonates between the concave shape of the barrel vault and the convex space embraced by the vault.

108. "A fifth interval reverberates between the vertical lines of the composite pillars and the empty three dimensional space they embrace."

109. "The sixth interval sounds in the relationship between the square of the floor and the rounded space created by the vaults."

110

110. "The seventh interval resonates between the concave shape of the barrel vault and the convex space embraced by the vault."

111

Triangles, rectangles, arches, columns, and garlands are not merely constructional or decorative elements but can be thought of as finely tuned instruments that allow the building to sound its harmonies. They are also more than an expression of the artist's personal style, as we can see by carefully examining the large canvas to the right of the high altar: *The Last Supper.* Although the work of another artist, Jacopo Tintoretto, it is, like the architecture of Andrea Palladio, conceived around a triangular structure.

The upper point of the triangle is to be found in the lamp shedding light on the scene. Out of the lamp's glow the "spiral of life" evolves: at first ethereal beings similar to thoughts appear, then human beings, such as the woman in the foreground taking dishes from a basket and, finally, the animals watching her. The base of the triangle is formed by the edge of the table. The right corner is marked by the figure of Christ rising from his seat.

111. *The Last Supper* by Jacopo Tintoretto.

112. *The Last Supper* is conceived in terms of a triangular structure.

112

What is missing in Tintoretto's painting is the third corner of the triangle. If we walk toward the Basilica's main altar looking at the painting at our side, the impression is that the left corner of the triangle is transcending the boundaries of the canvas; the arm of the triangle is reaching toward us, the spectators. Thus a living human being, the spectator, becomes the third point of the triangle.

In essence, the lamp at the upper point of the triangle denotes the source of all existing life forms. The second point, indicated by the Christ figure, marks the individuality of each living being. The third point of this trinity, personified by the spectator, celebrates the presence of life, here and now.

113 ▶

113. "Thus a living human being, the spectator, becomes the third point of the triangle."

The Redentore

114

Like the Basilica of San Giorgio Maggiore, the Redentore Basilica reveals itself outwardly as an architectonic construct and to our inner feeling as a pattern composed of a multitude of vibrations. As we visit the Redentore, we shall take a step further into the subtle reality of energies, a dimension almost unknown to our present civilization, which focuses its interests and investigations on concrete, physical phenomena.

114. The Redentore Basilica.

115. "We are not following an imaginary axis of the Redentore, but a vibrating stream of Earth energy ..."

When we explained the city's earth axis, we came across the telluric streams of energy known to us traditionally as "ley-lines" and to the Chinese as "dragon lines." They are thought to permeate the geological Earth close to its surface, distributing life energy over our planet. All life forms present on the planet, whether plant, animal or human, absorb this energy, and thus their growth, fertility and health are enhanced.

For this reason the ancient builders of cities, temples or churches sought, often subconsciously, to align their urban and architectural structures with this flow of earth energies. They were seeking to enrich their creation with the earth's radiation for the benefit of those who would for centuries walk the city streets or take part in religious rituals.

A trace of this influence of the earth's energies will be found at the Redentore if we study the direction of the Basilica's main axis. As with all sanctuaries, the direction in which it is aligned is one of its distinguishing marks. When we look at the Redentore from the shore in front of the Doges' Palace, we feel the Basilica is indeed facing in a certain direction. Let us try to follow this direction through the city.

115

116

116. Details of the façade of the Redentore Basilica.

116

117

The axis line first crosses the Giudecca Canal and then the Grand Canal, but while crossing the latter something unforeseen occurs. We have the strong impression that the axis line begins to turn right! Clearly we are not following an imaginary axis of the Redentore, but a vibrating stream of earth energy upon which the axis of the Redentore was placed with great precision. This means that the axis line is not limited to the ground on which the Basilica stands, but extends along the telluric current, toward the Adriatic Sea on one side and toward Central Europe on the other.

As we emphasized in connection with the Redentore's axis line, earth energy currents do not flow in straight lines only. They often wind and intersect, forming a network of energy streams all over the globe. The points where two or more of these currents meet and intersect are called "power points," because when the energy streams meet each other, they "open" and "spill" their magnetic power into the surrounding ground and atmosphere.

117. "The cupola's vault, encircled by three semi-cupolas, arches directly above this energy center."

The builders of temples or churches have always been drawn to locate their buildings upon these power points, which are permanently magnetized by beneficent radiation. Following their intuition and often using methods of divination that were secretly handed down from one generation of architects to the next, they made an effort to locate the most important part of a building precisely at the point where the telluric currents cross.

So the architect Andrea Palladio placed the longitudinal and the transverse axes of the Redentore Basilica upon two intersecting energy streams, positioning the crossing point of the two axes upon the power point. The cupola's vault, encircled by three semi-cupolas, arches directly above this energy center. Thus the radiation being released at the crossing-point below finds a corresponding architectonic vessel above.

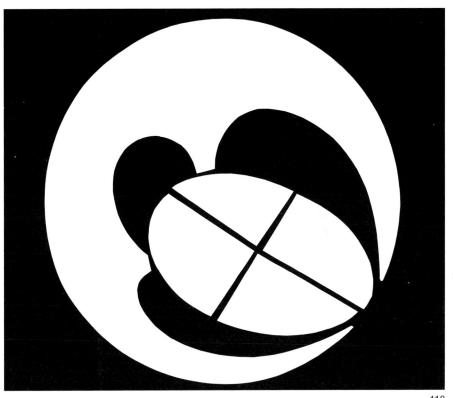

118

118. "The radiation being released at the crossing-point below finds a corresponding architectonic vessel above."

If we follow eastward the telluric energy stream on which the Redentore's transverse axis is placed, we discover that it also runs beneath the other two basilicas built by Palladio, San Giorgio Maggiore and San Pietro di Castello.

The three basilicas thus form a unique triad: outwardly all three are architectonic constructs, while inwardly they reveal a pattern of "sound." Each, however, "sounds" its own variation of the same melody. Although each basilica's longitudinal axis is placed along a different telluric current (I, II, III) crossing Venice's territory, all three are connected by a fourth energy stream (IV): the one we have detected beneath the transverse axis of the Redentore.

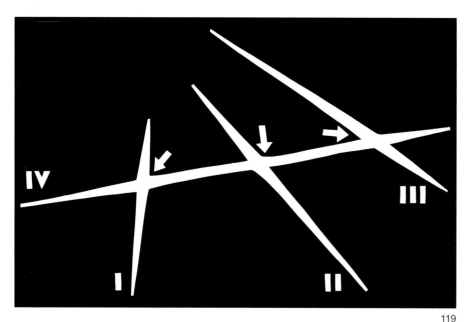

119

119. "Although each basilica's longitudinal axis is placed along a different telluric current (I, II, III) ... all three are connected by a fourth energy stream (IV) ..."

Looking at the map of Venice, we notice that the three basilicas aligned with these energy currents forms a slightly curved line shielding the city core around Saint Mark's Basilica and the Doges' Palace. This line runs almost parallel to the narrow strip of land to the southeast, the Lido. Just as the Lido protects Venice's lagoon from the open sea, we may assume that the line of basilicas protects the city at the psychic level.

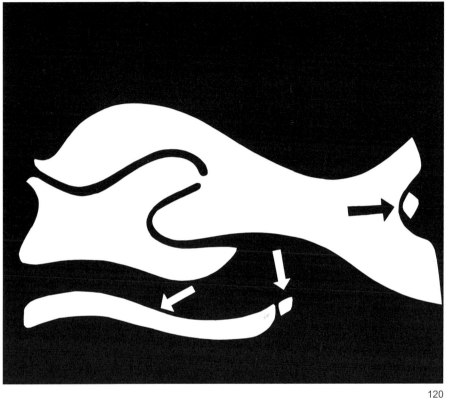

120

120. "Looking at the map of Venice, we notice that the three basilicas form a slightly curved line shielding the city core..."

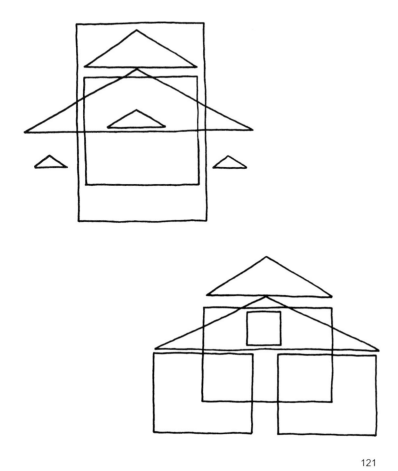

As we intuited, the vibrations emitted by the three basilicas have the character of sound patterns. These travel along the telluric energy stream connecting the three locations and form a *barrier of sound*. We can imagine that, when approaching Venice from the open sea, one would have to pass through this barrier. Let us suppose that each human being also emits vibrations, similar to musical sounds, which reflect emotional and mental states. If so, when crossing this barrier of sound, one's mental and emotional vibrations would subconsciously become attuned to the harmonious "sounds" emitted by the three basilicas. Thus attuned, one may step straight into the core of Venice, into Saint Mark's Square.

121

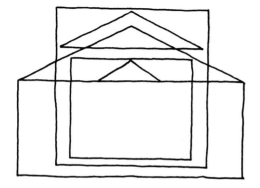

121. The "sound patterns" of the façades of San Pietro di Castello, San Giorgio Maggiore, and the Redentore basilicas.

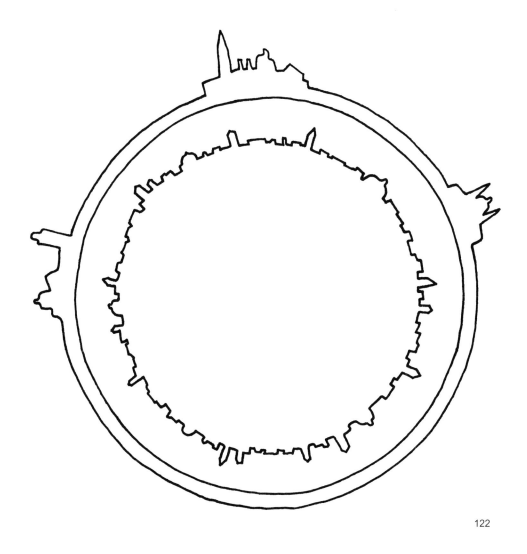

122

122. The "sound patterns" travel along the telluric energy stream connecting the three locations and form a barrier of vibrations shielding the city.

THE LIFE CURRENTS
OF VENICE

The Rialto Bridge

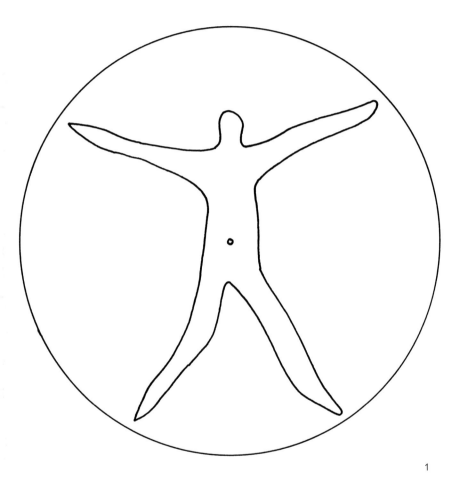

1

In the first part of this book we examined the core of Venice and found that the basic pattern of the city is preserved there, just as the shape of an entire tree is present in its seed.

In the second part we concentrated on the numerous buildings making up the body of Venice. We discovered that different structures embody cosmic and terrestrial energies and that these energies have vibrated for centuries within the organism of the city just as thoughts reverberate in the human mind.

We shall now examine the life currents of Venice, which have been flowing continuously for over a thousand years, keeping the city alive. As a river gradually shapes its bed, so these currents have gradually imprinted their presence upon the city. Canals, streets, bridges, squares, wells, gondolas and works of art bear the most tangible witness to them.

1. The Rialto Bridge is to the city of Venice as the navel is to the human body.

2. The Rialto Bridge is the point of balance of the city organism.

2

3

3. "The Rialto Bridge ... accentuates the waterway as the main thoroughfare of the 'water city'."

4

5

4. Traffic on the Grand Canal near the Bridge.

5. Further from the Bridge pedestrians are ferried across the Canal.

6

7

The spiritual center of Venice at Saint Mark's is complemented by the commercial center of the Rialto: together they form a complete unit. During the first centuries of Venice's existence, the offices of the city government were located in the Rialto area, and it was here that the commerce between East and West, the source of Venice's prosperity, flourished.

Originally a wooden bridge spanned the Grand Canal at the Rialto, the spot which we referred to earlier as "the navel of the city." After this bridge collapsed, the City decided to erect a stone bridge. Projects for the new construction were submitted by the greatest architects of the time: Michelangelo, Palladio, Sansovino and others. The project finally chosen was that of Antonio da Ponte who built the bridge between 1588 and 1591. The Rialto Bridge accurately embodies the character of Venice. It rises in an arch from both banks of the Grand Canal in a manner that accentuates the waterway as the main thoroughfare of the "water city." The elevated arch of the Bridge is lined with rows of small shops whose presence adds to the life flow upon it.

6. San Bartolomeo Square, at one end of the Rialto Bridge, becomes alive in the evening as the meeting place of young Venetians.

7. At the other end of the Bridge a street market is open day and night.

8

8. "The elevated arch of the Bridge is lined with rows of small shops …"

9

On the western wall of the Rialto Bridge is sculpted a sign that we shall meet again and again as we follow the life currents of Venice: the Annunciation. We have already come across this image in San Sebastiano where the Archangel and Mary, painted on opposite sides of the triumphal arch, communicate across the sanctuary.

On the Rialto Bridge we find the Archangel sculpted on one bank of the Grand Canal and Mary on the other. A steady stream of life flows to and fro across the bridge, and with it the words of their conversation. Let us compare this image with the ancient Greek image of the River Styx and its two banks: on one side is the material world as we know it from our daily experience, on the other, its invisible counterpart, the "kingdom of the soul," which we can understand today as a realm where human beings appear in energy form. Like Charon, who ferried souls from one side of the Styx to the other, the Rialto Bridge "ferries" people from one bank to the other.

9

9. "On the Rialto Bridge we find the Archangel sculpted on one bank of the Grand Canal and Mary on the other."

The Archangel represents the creative forces working from beyond the physical realm, the Virgin Mary their manifestation in daily reality, and the Bridge the link between the two. The image of the Annunciation therefore reveals Venice as a twofold being, bridging two complementary worlds and creating a balanced interflow between them.

The Annunciation appears on the Rialto Bridge and at a number of other focal points in the city. At Saint Mark's it crowns the façade of the Basilica in two turrets, one on each corner. The left-hand turret bears a sculpture of the Archangel, the right-hand one a sculpture of Mary.

We shall call the Annunciation the "secret symbol of Venice" to distinguish it from the official heraldic symbol, the winged-lion, itself also a twofold being: a bird-lion.

◀ 10

10. "We shall call the Annunciation the 'secret symbol of Venice' to distinguish it from the official heraldic symbol, the winged-lion..."

11. A medieval sculpture of the winged-lion is preserved in the Correr Museum.

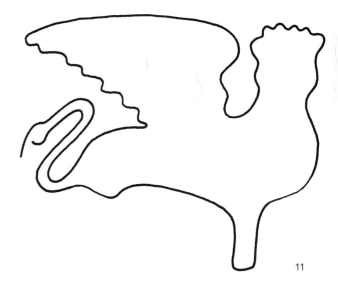

Canals, Streets and Bridges

12

The twofold nature of Venice is expressed in the structure of the city by a dual system of thoroughfares. Any part of the city can be reached either by boat on the canals or by walking through the streets.

There is a sense of balance between the system of waterways and the terrestrial thoroughfares, which can be inwardly experienced as the balance between the emotional and mental counterparts of our psychic world.

The waters of the canals are connected to the open sea, their rhythmic ebb and flow touching the banks of Venice's canals as well as distant ocean shores. Similarly, the emotional network of our psyche is structured in such a way that each tiny emotion vibrates throughout our entire being. On the other hand, each thought has a specific place in the framework of our mental world just as each street has a beginning, a direction, and an end.

12. The Sanctuary of Santa Maria dei Miracoli rises from the passing canal.

13. "There is a sense of balance between the system of waterways and the terrestrial thoroughfares ..."

13

13

13

13

14. The network of canals creates an emotional vibration throughout the city.

The bridges are the key points where the *mental* and the *emotional* thoroughfares of the city meet. When crossing a bridge, we become aware that all parts of the city are also interconnected by water. When gliding in a boat beneath the arch of a bridge, we become conscious of the other reality of Venice: the network of streets walked by pedestrians.

15

15. "The bridges are the key points where the mental and the emotional thoroughfares of the city meet."

16. "Beneath the arch of a bridge..."

17

Walking the streets of Venice or taking a boat through its canals are both experienced as something purposeful and very beautiful. We feel as though we are moving along streams of vibrant energy.

When visiting the Redentore Basilica we came across streams of energy: two telluric currents which cross beneath the intersection of the Basilica's axes. The energy of these streams, which we called the "life force" when visiting San Sebastiano Sanctuary, is the life bearing element of the Earth body. The human body has analogous streams of energy flowing through it which are used by the medical art of acupuncture in healing.

17. The constant passage of human beings creates another network of energy streams throughout the city.

In their design of the streets and canals and in their use of them for centuries, the Venetians have created yet another network of energy streams throughout the city — a micro-structure of personal streams of energy that we shall call "track lines," as they follow the tracks left by human beings.

18

18. "Walking the streets of Venice ..."

19. The network of narrow pedestrian streets is one reality of Venice.

20 ▶

20. When crossing a bridge we notice the other reality of Venice: all parts of the city are interconnected by water.

Wells and Gondolas

21

The terrestrial thoroughfares of Venice terminate in squares known as "campi." On each square we usually find a church and at least one family palace: yet another representation of the spiritual and material poles of the city. On each square stands a well: the wet element of water is present in an otherwise *dry* "campo."

The waterways converge in the Grand Canal, which is also lined with both churches and palaces. In the *wet* canal the *dry* element is present in the form of boats, in particular the traditional Venetian gondola.

Let us call to mind the yin–yang symbol of Chinese philosophy. The symbol is divided into two parts by a curve similar to that of the Grand Canal. One part is black, the other is white. In the black part there is a white dot, and in the white part there is a black dot. The opposites are not only separated but also interconnected. Similarly, in Venice, within the terrestrial square we find a dot of water, a well, and within the waterway there is a dot of solid matter, a gondola.

22

21. "In the *wet* canal the *dry* element is present in the form of boats ..."

22. "... within the terrestrial square we find a dot of water, a well ..."

23

23. "The terrestrial thoroughfares of Venice terminate in squares ..." such as the Campo San Polo.

220   VENICE: DISCOVERING A HIDDEN PATHWAY

24. "The waterways converge in the Grand Canal ... "

25

Today the wells of the Venetian squares are unused; instead, water is supplied directly to houses. The wells or "fontane" are preserved only as beautiful stone sculptures. In former times, when water was fetched by women, the wells were the actual centers of life in the squares.

The gondolas on the canals have also lost their original use as the principal means of transport in Venice. They sway by the banks of the canals like elegant wooden sculptures. There is a difference however: the wells are locked, while the gondolas may still be hired for trips.

25. "The wells … are preserved only as beautiful stone sculptures."

26. Though no longer a source of water, the wells are still a
focus of life in the square.

27

We have said that the gondola is a dot of solid matter — *the earth element* — within a waterway — *the water element*. The gondola's pointed prow and stern always bear the same two adornments, one resembling an "F" and the other an "S." Both curve high into the air, evoking *the air element*. *The fire element* is present in the dynamics of motion, which have resulted in the elegant design of oar and gondola: since the gondolier uses only a single oar to propel and steer the boat, the gondola itself must be rounded out on the opposite side to stabilize the direction of movement.

The gondola, like Saint Mark's Square, has been shaped through the centuries by the collective genius of Venice. Both are popular symbols of Venice. Both embody the elements of earth, water, air and fire. It would seem then that all four elements have played a decisive role in shaping the personality of Venice.

27. "... the gondola is a dot of solid matter — *the earth element* — within a waterway ..."

28. The "F" shape of the gondola's prow.

29. The gondola, like Saint Mark's Square, embodies the elements of earth, water, air and fire.

The Role of Art

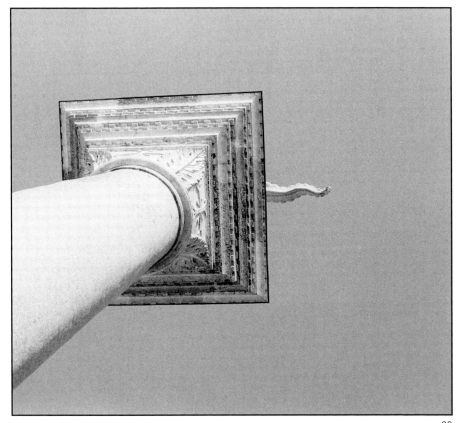

30

We are constantly discovering that Venice, in all its manifestations, is a city of carefully balanced opposites. We have talked about the earth dragon and the celestial winged-lion on the columns of the Venetian Portal. We have called attention to the balance between the sanctuaries embodying the spiritual pole, and the palaces embodying the material pole of the city. We have examined the balance between the streets and the waterways, which form the city's network of thoroughfares.

30. "We have talked about the earth dragon and the celestial winged-lion on the columns of the Venetian Portal."

30

31

Life dwells, however, not only in opposing poles and in the relationship that exists between them, but also in the medial form created when opposites unite in synthesis. Art is the most explicit medial form. Let us consider the art of painting. Here the material presence of colors and the spiritual content of the message merge into one indivisible whole.

The original value of a painting is determined not only by its colors nor by its message, but also by the painting's original location within the city organism. Today, when we look at paintings by Venetian masters scattered in European and American galleries, we can hardly imagine that each of these works of art had its own specific place within the body of Venice, where it remained for centuries, vibrating mysteriously with its architectonic and spiritual environments.

31. The water carrier, the symbol of synthesis, from a mosaic in Saint Mark's Basilica.

Titian's painting, the *Assunta*, depicting the ascent of the Virgin Mary into heaven, still hangs in its original place above the main altar of the Frari Church. Just as the Gothic interior of the Church is articulated on three levels, one above the other, so is the composition of the Renaissance painting.

In the Church, the lowest space, reaching up to shoulder level, is encircled by a massive wreath linking us with the material world. In Titian's painting this level is reflected in the dense group of human figures at the bottom.

In the second level of the Church, the walls are rendered almost transparent by numerous pointed windows through which a dazzling brightness penetrates. The elaborate lace-like edging of the windows and the stained glass tell us that this is the level of the spiritual world, which we can experience only in awesome silence. In Titian's *Assunta* the second level is also bathed in dazzling brightness and is encircled by the interlacing of supernatural beings. The people below can aspire to this level only with their eyes and gestures.

32

32. *"Titian's painting, the Assunta … still hangs in its original place above the main altar of the Frari Church."*

33

33. "The walls ... end suddenly, while their ribs curve inward until they terminate at the keystone."

The walls with their pointed windows give the impression that they should continue into infinity, but human creativity cannot reach that far. The walls, therefore, end suddenly, while their ribs vault inward until they terminate at the keystone. Thus, at the top of the Gothic sanctuary, otherwise directed toward the light, the third level is formed: a dark area, the vaulted ceiling.

The third level of Titian's *Assunta* is also sealed in darkness. Although the light tends to spread upward from the central level of the painting, it is halted by the darkened figure of the Father. The part where we would expect the brightest light to be appears dark, as in the Gothic sanctuary. The furthest dimensions of life are mysteriously hidden and elude our perception.

The Renaissance painting, which was placed on the main altar on March 20, 1518, parallels and echoes the Gothic sanctuary completed a century before.

Near the eastern edge of the city, in the Madonna dell' Orto Sanctuary, we find a similar situation.

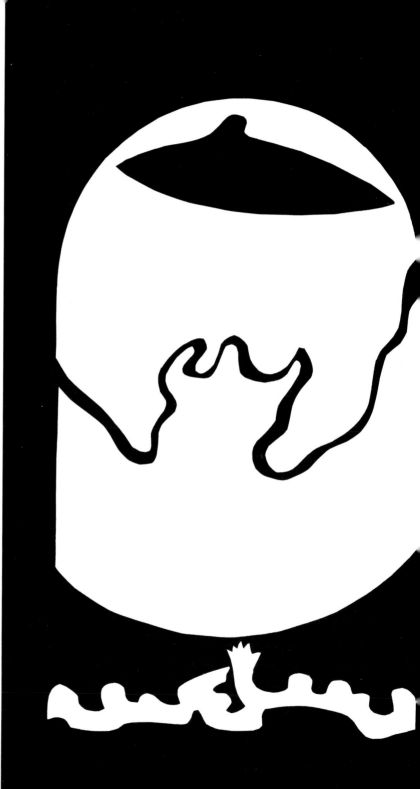

34. The three levels of Titan's painting, the *Assunta*.

35

Although the Sanctuary is built in the Gothic style, the Valier Chapel to the left of the nave was added later in the early Renaissance style. The forms of the Chapel, based on spheres, triangles and squares, are purely geometric. Here we find a painting of the same period (1480), Giovanni Bellini's *Madonna with an Angel*. The pale colors of the painting are in perfect harmony with the clean lines of the Chapel. Although the painting and the ambience are both extremely simple, they accentuate each other and enhance each other's expressive power, making the Chapel resound with intense vibration. A number of the "better" Bellini Madonnas can be found in the Academy Galleries but, having been removed from their original "home," none of them has the expressive power of the modest Madonna in the Valier Chapel.

35. The Madonna dell' Orto Sanctuary, home of Bellini's *Madonna with an Angel*.

It is not only a question of the stylistic relationship between the painting and its environment, for the latter could be reconstructed in a gallery and even transported across the ocean, but also of the relationship between the painting and the energy field for which it was conceived and in which it was embedded.

36. Titian's *Annunciation* in San Salvador Sanctuary, seen from the direction of the energy current with which it is aligned.

36

So far, we have mentioned two types of earth energy currents: one in connection with the axes of the Redentore Basilica and the other in relation to the city's thoroughfares. There exists yet a third type of energy currents. These come into being at the point where the magnetic power of a major line "opens" and "spills" into the ground or the atmosphere. They are called "aquastats." Their fixed courses often run along playful lines as if they were dancing through the earth, air or water. They lend depth to the physical ambience and create an energy pattern to which a painting can readily relate.

A good example can be found in Titian's *Annunciation* painted for one of the side altars of San Salvador Sanctuary. Our attention is attracted by a cone of light in the painting, which has its source in the opening between the angels and the clouds. The rays fall past both figures in the direction of the aquastat running through the interior of the Sanctuary. The light in the painting and the energy of the aquastat converge at one point only, but it is sufficient to permit this valuable energy to penetrate our consciousness with the same force today as it did centuries ago.

◀ 37

37. "The rays fall past both figures in the direction of the aquastat running through the interior of the Sanctuary."

38. The Scuola Grande della Misericordia.

The "Scuole"

39

The paintings in Venice not only adorned the many churches and palaces but also the numerous buildings of the lay confraternities called "scuole." People who belonged to the same profession or nationality, or shared the same interests, united themselves in a scuola. Each scuola was housed in its own building, divided into two halls, one above the other, each with its own altar in the manner of a church. A scuola was, however, essentially different from a church, which, no matter how intricately it may be extended horizontally or vertically, has only *one major all-embracing space*. The structure of a scuola also differed from a family palace, which has *any number of halls* to meet the innumerable needs and facets of life.

39. The two storeys of the Scuola Grande di San Rocco.

A scuola always had two halls, an upper one and a lower one, to symbolize its dual purpose: to serve on the spiritual as well as on the material level. We may assume that the members of a scuola "learned" how to make use of their spiritual awareness in their daily life. This is why each scuola had its own altars as well as sufficient space to shelter the sick and the hungry in times of epidemic, thus applying spiritual principles to human needs.

The Venetian scuole represent the medial element in the city's fabric, a bridge between the churches and the palaces. Since we have recognized art as a medial form too, it is not surprising that the scuole were important patrons of Venetian painting.

40

41

40. The upper hall of the Scuola Grande di San Rocco.

41. "A scuola always had two halls, an upper one and a lower one, to symbolize its dual purpose ..."

42

43

The majority of the scuole did not survive beyond the nineteenth century and their patrimony of paintings has been dispersed. The Scuola Grande della Carità underwent an interesting transformation preserving the traditional link between the scuole and Venetian painting: together with the former Church of Santa Maria della Carità and its monastery, it forms the premises of the present Academy which houses an important collection of paintings by Venetian masters.

In the hospice of the former Scuola, Titian's painting *The Presentation of the Virgin in the Temple* is preserved in its original place. Mary's parents and escorts are gathered at the foot of the staircase that runs diagonally across the painting. Mary is ascending the steps on her own, as a frail little girl. She has left her parents behind and is tentatively taking her first steps into independent life. There is no one to guide her. The path is lit only by the soft light of her own being: the whole of Mary's figure glows slightly. Waiting at the top are the masters, men who have already walked the distance now before the girl in blue, and who have already achieved the highest spiritual ideals.

42. "The glow around Mary has an *egg-like* form."

43. "At the bottom of the staircase sits an old woman between a dead chicken and a basket *full of eggs.*"

The glow around Mary has an *egg-like* form. At the bottom of the staircase sits an old woman between a dead chicken and a *basket full of eggs!* The direction in which Mary is walking leads from the dead chicken toward the basket of eggs. Leading from death to new life, this is an image of re-birth that is further accentuated by Mary's gesture: her left hand breaking out of the egg-form surrounding her.

In order to progress in initiation it is necessary to pass a test. This is emphasized in the painting by the old woman seated midway between death and life. The tip of her shawl is pointing exactly at the bottom of the step that Mary has just left behind. This old woman personifies the "silent guardian" of the eternal truth that there is no final death but only the ever potential re-birth of life.

44

44. The central part of Titian's painting *The Presentation of the Virgin in the Temple.*

This precious painting has been vibrating for centuries in its original place, and the air seems imbued with its essence. It celebrates the path of individuation, a path that each one of us must sooner or later walk. Rather than just looking at this painting then, we should look through the painting into ourselves.

The other paintings were brought to the Academy from various Venetian churches, palaces, and scuole. Among them are a few that act as the illuminated consciousness of Venice, reflecting the city's self awareness. Their message is still valid even though they have been removed from their original environments.

Let us return to the first hall of the Academy, the upper hall of the Scuola della Carità, and look at the *Madonna della Misericordia* triptych, created in 1439 by Jacobello del Fiore. To the left and right of the head of the central Madonna are painted the Angel and Mary, each in its own small space. The words of their conversation run between the two separate spaces as they do between the two banks of the Grand Canal at the Rialto Bridge. Here the secret symbol of Venice appears again.

45

45. The *Madonna della Misericordia* triptych by Jacobello del Fiore.

It is equally important to give attention to the larger figure of Mary. She does not hold Christ in her lap as other Madonnas do: he glows on her breast as the center of her being. The painting suggests that Christ is not a being distinct from Mary, but is her own inner self: the potential for perfection which we all carry within us.

In Saint Mark's Basilica there is another Madonna, conceived in a similar way, exhibited in a place of honor and surrounded with jewels. This is the ancient icon *Madonna Nicopeia*, brought home by the Venetians after the conquest of Constantinople in the thirteenth century and considered the talisman of Venice. Here, too, Christ appears at the place where we locate our deepest self, in the heart.

46

46. The *Madonna Nicopeia* in Saint Mark's Basilica.

Given the significance attributed to the *Madonna Nicopeia*, we may assume that the roots of Venetian civilization were anchored in an awareness of the divine potential of each human being. This idea was expressed only in a veiled manner during the Middle Ages, when the two paintings were venerated, but it was openly asserted with the humanistic impulse prevailing in the following centuries. To a humanist, divinity does not exist outside oneself. Each man's or woman's deepest essence is divine.

◀ 47

47. In the icon of *Madonna Nicopeia* Christ appears in the place where we locate our deepest self.

48. Christ glows on the breast of the *Madonna della Misericordia* as the center of her being.

49

Among the paintings in the Academy collection the *Presentation of Christ in the Temple*, by Vittore Carpaccio, helps to deepen our knowledge of the essence of Venice. The painting portrays three women on the left and three men on the right. Between them a little Christ-child is being passed from hand to hand.

Once again we encounter the female and the male poles of life and "the bridge" that links them. This time, however, the emphasis is not on the two poles, but on the energy that bridges them: the child being passed from the hands of the women to the hands of the men.

From our previous meeting with the child in the "heart" of two Madonnas, we know that he represents our inner self, the perfect human being purified of selfishness and destructive inclinations — the ideal that we are continually striving to attain. Carpaccio's painting conveys the message that Venice has been carefully balancing the two poles, creating an ambience within which this ideal human being can develop.

49. The *Presentation of Christ in the Temple* by Vittore Carpaccio.

Carpaccio's painting reflects the essence of Venice so accurately that it can be translated directly into the visible structure of the city. If we compare the group of women to one bank of the Grand Canal and the group of men to the other, the body of the Christ-child can be interpreted as the Rialto Bridge.

The three angel musicians depicted along the bottom edge of the painting reflect the arrangement at the edge of the city of the three basilicas of Palladio sounding their inner melodies. Could it be that, listening to the angels' harmonies with our inner ear, we can distinguish the sounds of San Pietro di Castello, San Giorgio Maggiore and the Redentore?

50. The blending of inner melodies from Palladio's three basilicas echoes the harmony created by Carpaccio's three angel musicians.

Let us now turn to Giorgione's painting *The Tempest*, one of those rare works of art that affects us deeply for no apparent reason. Our interest in *The Tempest* may be so great because, through it, the mystery of our civilization, otherwise submerged deep in the collective unconscious, rises to the surface.

Through the center of the painting runs a stream of water. On the left bank stands a man, on the right bank sits a woman: yet another portrayal of the two poles of life. The standing male is holding an upright stick, the symbol of masculine power; the seated woman suggests a circular movement with her legs and is breast-feeding a baby, both symbols of female energies. Directly behind the man we see the ancient ruin of a man-made structure, while the woman is surrounded by luxuriant natural growth. Thus the two poles of creativity face each other. The male principle creates by imposing upon nature, the female by harmonizing with it.

◀ 51

51. "The two poles of creativity face each other." After *The Tempest* by Giorgione.

Thus far, the painting may be understood as an expression of our dualistic, bi-polar civilization that Venice throughout the centuries has been trying to harmonize and balance. But looking up, we are struck by the thundering sky. A feeling of dread emerges from the otherwise peaceful scene. This feeling is accentuated by the apparent alienation between the man and the woman.

The superior attitude of the man suggests the aggressiveness of the male pole with all its consequences of disrupted equilibrium that are so acutely felt today. What happened to Venice, a *female* city, is in this sense symbolic. The life of the Venetian Republic was ended by the *male* hand of Napoleon's militarism less than 300 years after Giorgione completed this work of art.

52. *The Tempest* by Giorgione.

52

53. In *The Annunciation* by Paolo Veronese, an image of an unusual temple, remote in time and space, appears between Mary and the Angel.

Let us consider one last painting, *The Annunciation* by Paolo Veronese, created for the former "Scuola dei Mercanti." Here the Angel and Mary do not stand on the opposite sides of the Grand Canal as they do at the Rialto Bridge. Instead, the image of an unusual temple, remote in time and space, appears between them.

At first little can be explained, but if we concentrate on the image of the temple in the background, a peculiar feeling — perhaps of some ancient, scarcely known era — begins to stir in us. Indeed, we find ourselves wondering how a water civilization could spring up in the midst of an utterly different European culture? Is Venice perhaps the last remaining expression of some long-lost aquatic civilization?

54

54. A detail from *The Annunciation* by Veronese, showing the temple in the background in its entirety.

55

The feeling radiating from the center of Veronese's painting hints that Venice — a water city — is not a fortuitous phenomenon nor the arbitrary invention of the generations that built it, but is the result of thousands and thousands of years of experience previously gained in the creation of water civilizations. Perhaps the thread of these experiences originated in the era of Atlantis, the lost water civilization. A trace of this thread can still be perceived at the roots of classical Greek culture.

55. *The Annunciation* by Paolo Veronese.

The link between Venice and ancient civilizations is expressed in the painting by the three temples which recede one behind the other. The temple closest to us, housing the scene of the Annunciation, the "secret symbol of Venice," belongs to the Venetian era. The next, not far beyond, adorned by two figures representing the powers of the intellect, stands for classical Greek culture. The third temple is placed far back in the very center of the painting. Appearing there in its entirety, its windows are closed and its interior seems empty ... a far memory of a completely lost civilization, which could be identified as Atlantis.

Venice, then, conveys to our modern world the message of water civilizations that disappeared as a result of the increasing dominance on the planet of the male principle. The sensitively balanced beauty we encounter in Venice had been gathering strength gradually over millennia. We shall need to reinstate the feminine qualities if we wish to transform our modern male-oriented civilization and mold a new era of harmony and balance upon the planet.

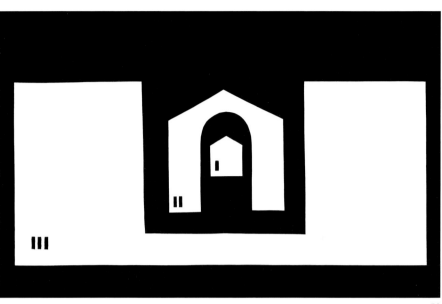

56

56. "The link between Venice and ancient civilizations is expressed ... by the three temples which recede one behind the other."

Glass

57

With the aid of art, we have descended deeper and deeper into the identity and origins of Venice. Let us now re-ascend to the surface.

The reflection of art is applied art, or handicrafts, many of which were developed to perfection in Venice. The most exquisite is glassmaking. A special center for glass workshops was established on the island of Murano to the east of Venice. The island is a miniature replica of Venice with its own little "Grand Canal," and its Romanesque basilica, Santa Maria e Donato.

Some of the glass workshops are open to the public and one can watch the masters at work. The shapeless mass of glass is aglow. From time to time the master blows into it through a long pipe and touches it with cold objects, thus allowing it to harden into the required shape.

57. The island of Murano is a special center for glassmaking.

Such a description is, however, hardly adequate. If we follow the process carefully with the eye of the imagination, we shall not be surprised to find a link with the secret symbol of Venice as represented on the Rialto Bridge. As the glowing mass of fluid glass acquires a firm shape, the light imprisoned within it (the Angel) is crystallized into matter (the Virgin Mary). The glass worker's breath is the bridge (the Rialto) across which the spark flashes from one dimension of reality to the other. This is the same spark that flashes between the two columns of the City Portal on Saint Mark's Little Square.

Glass is the most suitable substance through which the essential nature of Venice can be expressed. Glass, more than any other material substance, conjures up the living presence of light. Looking at it, we experience within ourselves the transitional moment just before light "hardens" into matter.

When we experience Venetian glass we experience the essence of Venice. Venice floats between light and matter, between Cosmos and Earth. It touches both, floating in the space between the two.

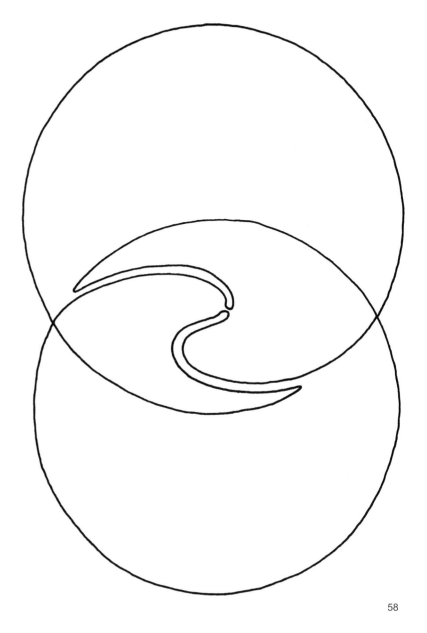

58

58. "Venice floats between light and matter, between Cosmos and Earth."

59. "Glass... conjures up the living persence of light."

60. "When we experience Venetian glass we experience
the essence of Venice."

About the Book

Marko Pogačnik, has had a growing relationship with Venice since 1979 when he led his first workshop there entitled "The Art of Growth." During that workshop he presented the Basilica of Santa Maria della Salute as a living work of art related not only to its historical context, but primarily to the path of our personal growth here and now. Successive seminars and lectures provided additional material over the years.

Bojan Brecelj has accompanied Marko in his explorations of Venice from the very beginning, and his photographs in this book capture in a visual medium the sensitive relationships intuited by Marko.

About the Authors

Marko Pogačnik was born in 1944 in Kranj, Slovenia. In 1965, after graduating from the Academy of Fine Arts in Ljubljana, Slovenia, he started his artistic activity as a founding member of the OHO group, working closely with contemporary conceptual and land-art movements. The group exhibited in the art museums of the former Yugoslavia and also in Florence, Munich, and Paris. In 1970 they were invited by the Museum of Modern Art in New York to take part in the international show "Information."

In 1971 with the aim of linking artistic creativity with the everyday life, Marko, his wife Marika, and their friends founded a small rural community and art group called "The Šempas family." Settling in an old farm house at Šempas in the Vipava valley close to the western border of Slovenia, they explored biodynamic agriculture, modern spiritual movements, and the ideals of community living. The community developed its artistic expression through sculptures-mobiles created from clay, wood, wool, and iron. Their work was presented at the Venice Biennale in 1978.

In 1979 Marko started to develop methods of what he calls "Earth Healing" and "Geomancy." Geomancy can be understood as a form of holistic ecology whereby not only the visible elements of the landscape play an important role, but also its consciousness (elemental beings), vital-energy streams and centers, its soul essence, and its spiritual dimensions (the landscape temple). Marko's Earth healing work began in the mid 80s when he developed a method of Earth acupuncture that he calls "lithopuncture." During a lithopuncture project, columns of local stone are permanently positioned on chosen spots in a city or landscape to act as acupuncture needles. A "cosmogram" is carved on each one. Cosmograms are signs of identity that are active in guiding life forces and focusing spiritual qualities.

Lithopuncture works include:

Lithopuncture of two castle parks in Türnich (1986–89) Cappenberg, Germany (1988–92)

Lithopuncture of the territory on both sides of the border between North Ireland and Republic of Ireland, Orchard Gallery, Derry (1991–92)

Lithopuncture of the urban ambiences of Villach (1995), Klagenfurt (1998), and Bad Radkersburg, Austria (2001); Nova Gorica, Slovenia (2001-02); Quito, Ecuador (2003); St. Veit, Austria (2004); Zagreb, Croatia (2004); Prague, Czech Republics (2005-06); Bad Pyrmont, Germany (2006)

"Alpenstern," a cross-Alps lithopuncture project with lithopuncture stones in Italy (Merano), Austria (Villach), Slovenia (Maribor, Bohinj) and Germany (Chiemsee) (1997)

Lithopuncture of Circuito das Aguas landscape, Minas Gerais, Brazil (1998)

Seeland lithopuncture network, Switzerland (1998-2002)

Aachen lithopuncture network, Ludwig Forum Aachen, Germany (1999)

Geopuncture stone circle "Solar Plexus of Europe," Zagreb, Croatia (2005)

In 1991 Marko Pogačnik designed a cosmogram for the official coat of arms and the flag of the newly constituted Republic of Slovenia.

Books by Marko Pogačnik,

Ley-lines and Ecology (together with William Bloom, 1985)
Nature Spirits and Elemental Beings (1996)
Healing the Heart of the Earth (1998)
Christ Power and the Earth Goddess (1999)
Earth Changes, Human Destiny (2000)
The Daughter of Gaia (2001)
Turned Upside Down (2004)
So Wide the Heart (together with Ana Pogačnik, 2006)
Touching the Breath of Gaia (2007)
Venice: Discovering a Hidden Pathway (1986, 2007)
Sacred Geography: Co-creating the Earth Cosmos (2008)

Bojan Brecelj is the founder of an independent multimedia studio in Ljubljana, Slovenia, called IPAK – Photo Press Agency (www.ipak.si). He works with a variety of visual media: photography, graphic design, multivision, stage design, and video. From 1988 to 2002, he was a free-lance photojournalist for magazines worldwide, collaborating with Gamma, Still Pictures, Visum, Saola, Grazia Neri, Corbis, and Sygma. Bojan's interest is in both experimental and documentary photography in which a subject is always in relation to the environment, as well as sustainable development and its effects in society. Through the past twenty-five years he has collaborated in Earth healing projects with Marko and has created several presentations to complement Marko's workshops.